ENGLISH in Common 6B

Student Book/Workbook
with ActiveBook

JJ Wilson with Antonia Clare

Series Consultants
Sarah Louisa Birchley and María Victoria Saumell

ALWAYS LEARNING

PEARSON

English in Common 6B
Student Book/Workbook Split Edition

Pearson Education, 10 Bank Street, White Plains, NY 10606

Staff credits: The editorial, design, production, and manufacturing people who make up the *English in Common 6* team are Margaret Antonini, Allen Ascher, Rhea Banker, Eleanor Kirby Barnes, Peter Benson, Mike Boyle, Tracey Cataldo, Aerin Csigay, Mindy DePalma, Dave Dickey, Chris Edmonds, Mike Kemper, Jessica Miller-Smith, Laurie Neaman, Daria Ruzicka, Loretta Steeves, Jeff Zeter, and Charlie Green.

This series is dedicated to Charlie Green. Without Charlie's knowledge of pedagogy, strong work ethic, sense of humor, patience, perseverance, and creativity, *English in Common* would never have existed.

Cover design: Tracey Cataldo
Cover photo: © qushe/shutterstock.com
Text design: Tracey Cataldo
Text composition: TSI Graphics
Text font: MetaPlus

ISBN 13: 978-0-13-267894-0
ISBN 10: 0-13-267894-2

Library of Congress Cataloging-in-Publication Data
Bygrave, Jonathan
English in common. Book 1 / Jonathan Bygrave.
p. cm.
ISBN 0-13-247003-9—ISBN 0-13-262725-6—
ISBN 0-13-262727-2—ISBN 0-13-262728-0—
ISBN 0-13-262729-9—ISBN 0-13-262731-0
1. English language—Textbooks for foreign speakers.
2. English language—Grammar.
3. English language—Spoken English.
PE1128.B865 2011
428.24--dc23

2011024736

Student Book Photos Credits: All photos are used under license from Shutterstock.com except for the following: p. 71 (top) Dreamstime.com, (bottom) Dreamstime.com; p. 74 (top left) Bettmann/Corbis, (bottom middle left) Colorsport/Imago/Icon SMI/Newscom, (bottom middle right) Allstar Picture Library/Alamy, (bottom right) Shelley Gazin/Corbis; p. 76 (right) Pictorial Press Ltd/Alamy; p. 83 iStockphoto.com; p. 98 Jon Bradley/Getty Images; p. 103 (A) KRT/Newscom, (D) Photos 12/Alamy; p. 104 (left) iStockphoto.com, (middle) Danita Delimont/Alamy, (right) North Wind Picture Archives/Alamy; p. 106 (left) Lebrecht Music and Arts Photo Library/Alamy, (top) Pictorial Press Ltd/Alamy, (bottom) The Protected Art Archive/Alamy; p. 107 Zumapress.com/Newscom; p. 114 (left) Bettmann/Corbis, (right) Bettmann/Corbis; p. 115 (C) iStockphoto.com; p. 118 Courtesy of Doriet Chichester; p. 119 (bottom) Pictorial Press Ltd/Alamy; p. 126 (bottom right) iStockphoto.com; p. 135 (1) Chris Ware/The Image Works, (2) SuperStock/SuperStock, (3) Stewart Cook/Rex USA.

Workbook Photo Credits: All photos are © Pearson Education except for the following. Workbook p. 44 Shutterstock.com; Workbook p. 46 Shutterstock.com; Workbook p. 52 PA Photos/Landov; Workbook p. 54 (all) Shutterstock.com; Workbook p. 55 Shutterstock.com; Workbook p. 56 Shutterstock.com; Workbook p. 58 Shutterstock.com; Workbook p. 61 Shutterstock.com; Workbook p. 62 Shutterstock.com; Workbook p. 66 Shutterstock.com; Workbook p. 71 Time & Life Pictures/Getty Images; Workbook p. 73 Creatas/Punchstock; Workbook p. 74 Joe Raedle/Getty Images; Workbook p. 80 Shutterstock.com; Workbook p. 83 Shutterstock.com.

Illustration Credits: Beach (Beach-o-matic), Mark Duffin, Brian Lee, Sally Newton, Amanda Montgomery-Higham (SGA), Roger Penwill, and Lucy Truman (New Division)

Text Credits: Page 69, Audio 1.28 from "Sydney Harbour Bridge," Commonwealth of Australia, Australian Stories, http://australia.gov.au/about-australia/australian-story/sydney-harbour-bridge viewed July 30, 2011. This work constitutes copyright of the Commonwealth of Australia, http://australia.gov.au/about-australia/australian-stories and is licensed under a Creative Commons Attribution 3.0 Australia license, http://creativecommons.org/licenses/by/3.0/au/. Reprinted by permission. Page 122, from *The House on Mango Street* by Sandra Cisneros. Copyright © 1984 by Sandra Cisneros. Published by Vintage Books, a division of Random House, Inc., and in hardcover by Alfred A. Knopf in 1994. By permission of Susan Bergholz Literary Services, New York, NY and Lamy, NM and Bloomsbury Publishing. All rights reserved. Workbook Page 80, Excerpt from "Mine" reprinted with permission of Allen Ascher.

Printed in the United States of America
2 3 4 5 6 7 8 9 10—V082—16 15 14 13 12

Contents

Student Book

Workbook

English in Common is a six-level course that helps adult and young-adult English learners develop effective communication skills that correspond to the Common European Framework of Reference for Languages (CEFR). Every level of *English in Common* is correlated to a level of the CEFR, and each lesson is formulated around a specific CAN DO objective.

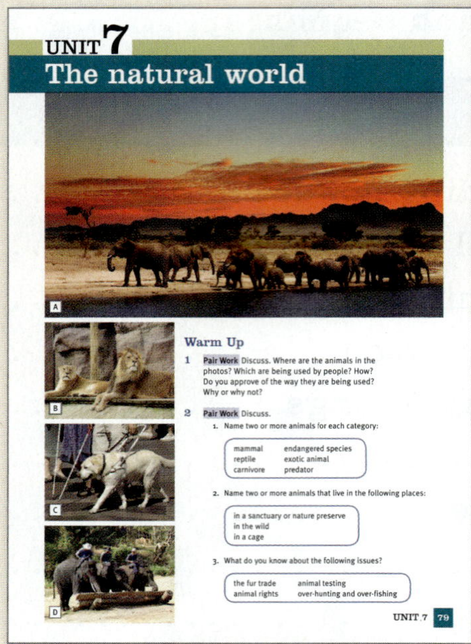

English in Common 6 has ten units. Each unit has twelve pages.

There are three three-page lessons in each unit.

A Unit Wrap Up ends each unit.

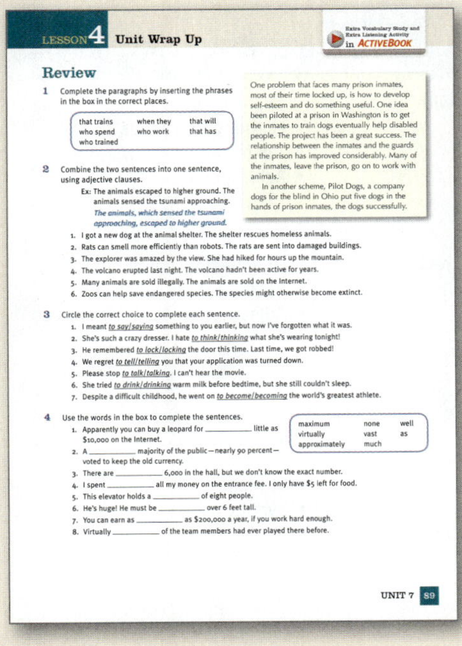

Back of Student Book

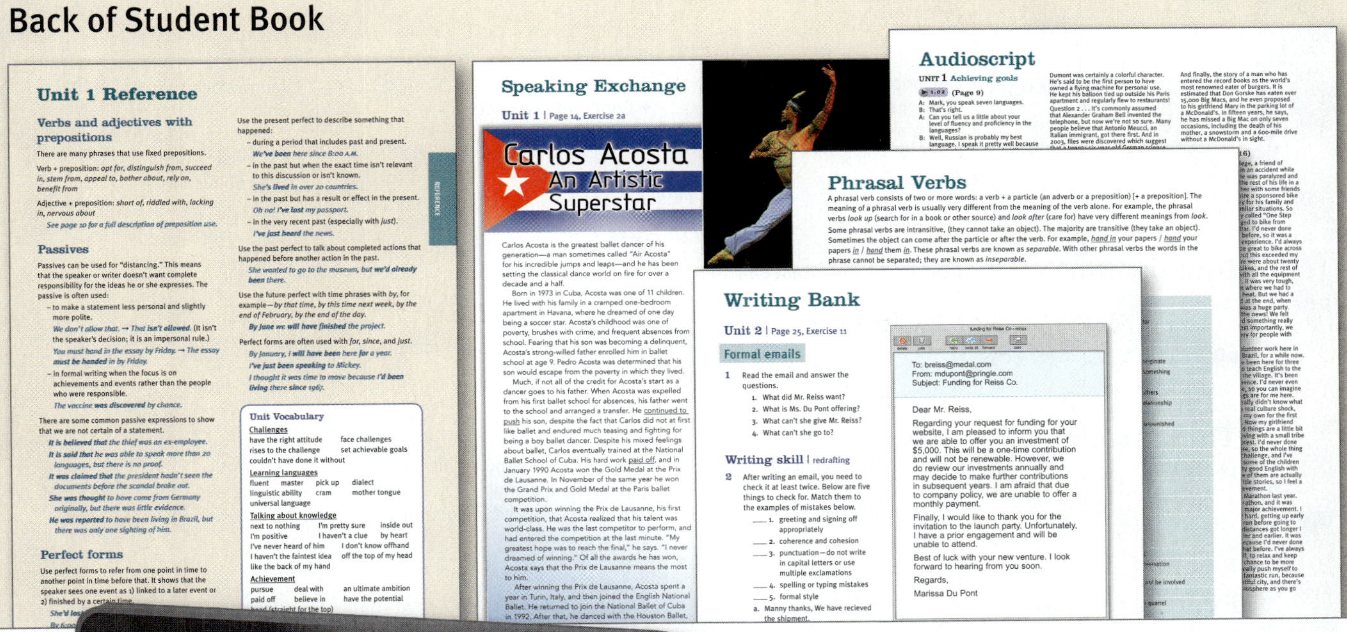

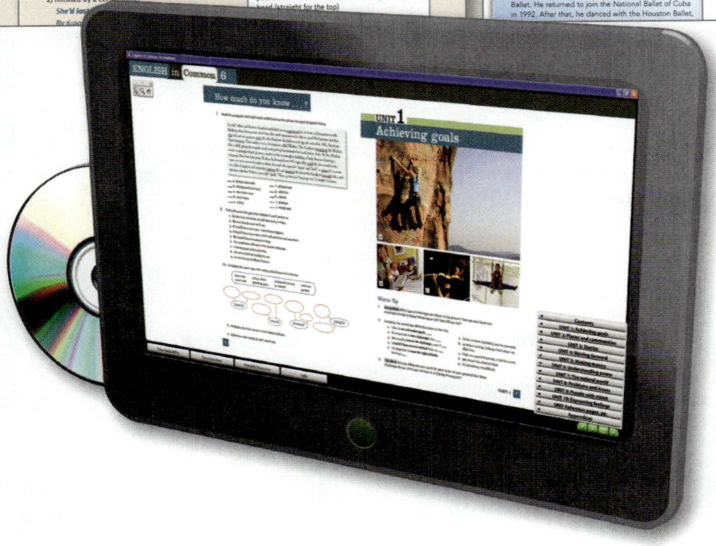

- Each Student Book contains an ***ActiveBook***, which provides the Student Book in digital format. *ActiveBook* also includes the complete Audio Program and Extra Listening activities.
- An optional online **MyEnglishLab** provides the opportunity for extra practice anytime, anywhere.
- The Teacher's Resource Book contains teaching notes, photocopiable extension activities, and an ***ActiveTeach***, which provides a digital Student Book enhanced by interactive whiteboard software. *ActiveTeach* also includes the videos and video activities, as well as the complete Test Bank.

READING/WRITING	LISTENING	COMMUNICATION/EXTRA VOCABULARY STUDY
Reading texts: • an article about polyglots • articles about two incredible athletes • a personality quiz **Writing task:** write a news report based on a picture	**Listening texts:** • an interview with a polyglot • a radio show about "famous firsts" • news stories • descriptions of personal achievements • analysis of answers to a personality quiz	**Communication:** take a personality quiz **Extra Vocabulary Study in *ActiveBook*:** prefixes
Reading texts: • an article about Wikipedia • formal emails • descriptions of travel destinations **Writing tasks:** • write recommendations for travelers to your country • write a formal email • write a description of a favorite place	**Listening texts:** • descriptions of life abroad • a debate over the value of the Internet • descriptions of two clubs to which people belong	**Communication:** collaborate on a plan **Extra Vocabulary Study in *ActiveBook*:** phrasal verbs
Reading texts: • an article about famous hoaxes • a biography of Groucho Marx **Writing task:** write a description of someone	**Listening texts:** • descriptions of favorite fictional characters • an abridged biography of Groucho Marx • a joke	**Communication:** tell a story **Extra Vocabulary Study in *ActiveBook*:** metaphors
Reading texts: • an article on scientifically generated "superpowers" • an article on child geniuses • descriptions of new technology **Writing task:** summarize a story from a listening	**Listening texts:** • news stories • a conversation about superheroes • an interview with the creator of Spider Man • telephone conversations about future plans • an interview about child geniuses • discussions about discoveries and inventions	**Communication:** make an argument for research funding **Extra Vocabulary Study in *ActiveBook*:** two-part expressions
Reading texts: • an article about a unique business model • true "riches to rags" stories • an article about famous philanthropists • an article about *Fortune* Magazine's 100 Best Companies to Work For **Writing task:** write a paragraph supporting an opinion	**Listening texts:** • advice on choosing a business partner • an interview with the CEO of a successful company • a discussion about a hypothetical business situation	**Communication:** negotiate **Extra Vocabulary Study in *ActiveBook*:** idioms 1
Reading texts: • an article on architecture as a symbol of power • an article about the power of charisma **Writing tasks:** • write about two important pieces of architecture • write an autobiographical statement	**Listening texts:** • descriptions of important architectural structures • an interview about the influence of teens on technology • conversations about limits on teenagers	**Communication:** evaluate personal characteristics **Extra Vocabulary Study in *ActiveBook*:** idioms 2
Reading texts: • an article on using animals to save human lives • an article about illegal online animal sales **Writing tasks:** • explain procedures in your home • write an ad for an object	**Listening texts:** • advice on choosing and caring for pets • a description of a travel adventure • a description of an unusual job • a discussion about how to develop a piece of land	**Communication:** reach a compromise on a plan **Extra Vocabulary Study in *ActiveBook*:** suffixes
Reading texts: • opinions on necessary future inventions • an "online" advice column **Writing tasks:** • write an essay on a problem or issue	**Listening texts:** • descriptions of imaginary inventions • explanations of career choices • conversations about problems with machines	**Communication:** summarize opinions on issues **Extra Vocabulary Study in *ActiveBook*:** academic English
Reading texts: • an article about famous visionaries • an article about fine art theft • advice for aspiring travel writers and photographers **Writing tasks:** • write about thoughts and actions inspired by a photo • write a story based on a hypothetical situation	**Listening texts:** • an interview about geniuses' "aha" moments • conversations about works of art • histories of two important inventors	**Communication:** collaborate on a proposal **Extra Vocabulary Study in *ActiveBook*:** confusing words
Reading texts: • an article about a blind photographer • a book review • an excerpt from a novel **Writing task:** write about a childhood memory	**Listening texts:** • an interview about optimism and pessimism • deductions about feelings in the past • recollections of childhood • explanations of strong opinions	**Communication:** express strong feelings about an issue **Extra Vocabulary Study in *ActiveBook*:** phrasal verbs and particles

UNIT 6

Understanding power

A

B

C

D

Warm Up

1 What types of "power" are represented in the photos? Create phrases by combining the words in the box with *power* or *powerful*. Then use five of your phrases in sentences.

Ex: *powerful speech* *The president gave a powerful speech last night.*

medicine	nuclear	speech	spending	argument	world	tool	army
influence	political	people	consumer	economic	reasons	brain	wind

2 **Pair Work** Check that you understand the phrases in bold. Discuss the questions.

1. Do you think people **have** enough **power over** the decisions that affect their lives?
2. Should more women be **in positions of power**?
3. Can you think of any countries that are growing in **economic power**?
4. In what circumstances should police be given **special powers**?
5. What political changes often occur when a new leader **comes to power**?

Describe an important building or structure

GRAMMAR articles

CAN DO

Reading

The Eiffel Tower

The Pentagon

The Forbidden City

1 **Pair Work** Discuss.

1. What is the most impressive building you have ever seen?
2. Do you generally prefer modern or traditional architecture? Give examples.
3. What is the most beautiful or ugliest building in your town or city? Are there any that you think should be torn down or restored?

2 Read the article.

The Architecture of Power

No one knew better than the Romans how to gain political influence through the use of engineering and architecture. The Romans built roads, bridges, aqueducts, forums, amphitheaters, and baths in order to win over the minds of the cultures they were conquering. It's hard not to be impressed by a power that provides you with clean water, a road to the capital city, a way to travel across previously impassable rivers, and incredible public buildings.

Architecture has played an important part in public life throughout history, whether as homage to an individual or as a monument to an institution or ideology.

Architecture has always been a potent symbol of wealth, status, and power. From castles to cathedrals, from the pyramids to skyscrapers, architecture has always served to glorify the ideal of the time.

Vocabulary | power

3 Use the words in the box to complete the definitions and example sentences. You may need to change the verb tenses.

win	gain	impressed	part	by	play	over	important	be

1. ___________: to obtain or achieve something
   We are hoping to ___________ a better understanding of the process.
2. ___________ ___________: to get someone's support or friendship by being nice to them
   The party worked hard to ___________ ___________ undecided voters.
3. ___________ ___________ ___________: feel admiration and respect for
   The CEO ___________ ___________ ___________ your presentation.
4. ___________ an ___________ ___________ in: to have a big effect or influence
   Everyone from the cleaners to the management ___________ an ___________ ___________ in this year's financial success.

The CN Tower

The Great Pyramid

Chan Chan

Sydney Harbor Bridge

4 **Pair Work** Discuss.

1. According to Exercise 2, how did the Romans use architecture to increase their power?
2. How has architecture been used through history?

Listening

5a Look at the photos and guess which structure:

1. allows visitors to see up to 120 kilometers away?
2. had a sophisticated irrigation system?
3. was constructed by 400,000 men?
4. is known as the "coathanger"?
5. takes 20 minutes to walk around?
6. is one of the largest palaces in the world?
7. was built in 1889?

b ▶1.28 Listen and check your answers.

6 **Pair Work** Which structures sound the most impressive or interesting to you? Which have you visited or would you like to visit?

Grammar | articles

7 Circle the correct choice to complete the rules in the Active Grammar box.

Active Grammar

1. Use a / an / the / no article to introduce something new or unexpected. It indicates that the reader or listener does not know what is being talked about.
   I just bumped into ____ old friend.
2. Use a / an / the / no article to indicate "common ground." It may refer the reader or listener to a shared experience or general knowledge. The context will be important to establish exactly which noun is being referred to.
   I went to see ____ house this morning. (I told you about this house. Shared experience.)
3. Use a / an / the / no article to refer to something in general.
   I enjoy talking to taxi drivers. (taxi drivers in general)

See Reference page 127

8 Write *a*, *an*, or *the* in each space or leave the space blank.

The Sagrada Familia in ______ (**1.**) Barcelona is one of ______ (**2.**) Antoni Gaudí's most impressive works. This enormous church, as yet unfinished, is in some respects ______ (**3.**) summary of everything that Gaudí designed before. ______ (**4.**) architectural style of the Sagrada Familia has been called "warped Gothic," and it's easy to see why. The contours of ______ (**5.**) stone façade make it look as though the Sagrada Familia is melting in ______ (**6.**) sun, while ______ (**7.**) towers are topped with brightly colored mosaics that look like ______ (**8.**) bowls of fruit. Gaudí believed that ______ (**9.**) color is life, and, knowing that he would not live to see ______ (**10.**) completion of his masterpiece, he left colored drawings of his vision for future architects to follow.

For nearly 30 years, Gaudí worked on the Sagrada Familia and other projects simultaneously, until 1911, when he decided to devote himself exclusively to ______ (**11.**) church. During ______ (**12.**) last year of his life, Gaudí lived in ______ (**13.**) studio at the Sagrada Familia.

Tragically, in June 1926, Gaudí was run over by ______ (**14.**) tram. Because he was poorly dressed, he was not recognized, and ______ (**15.**) taxi drivers refused to take a "bum" to the hospital (they were later fined by ______ (**16.**) police). Gaudí died five days later and was buried in the crypt of the building to which he had devoted 44 years of his life, ______ (**17.**) as yet unfinished Sagrada Familia.

Speaking

9 **Pair Work** Think of three more important buildings or structures. What do you know about them? Make notes. Then share your choices with the class and explain why you chose them.

I think the Great Wall of China is one of the most amazing structures in the world. It was built . . .

Writing

10a Choose two important buildings or structures that you know about. If possible, do some research to find out more information about them.

b Write a paragraph about each of the structures you have chosen, using phrases from the How To box, as appropriate.

c **Group Work** Read your paragraphs to other students. Which buildings or structures do you think have been most influential? Why?

How To:

Describe important architecture

Use superlatives	• *The Great Pyramid is* ***arguably the most*** *. . . ,* • *It is* ***one of*** *Australia's* ***best known****, and* ***most photographed*** *. . .* • *It is* ***the world's largest*** *. . .*
Use fronting for dramatic effect	• ***Built to house the body of a pharaoh,*** *the base of the Great Pyramid . . .* • ***Fondly known as the "coathanger,"*** *Sydney Harbor Bridge . . .*
Provide details (size, description, etc.)	• *It is* ***built from*** *iron/stones . . .* • ***Occupying/Covering an area of more than*** *. . . square meters* • ***Standing*** *134 meters* ***high/above*** *. . .*
Describe reason for building/purpose	• *It was* ***built to commemorate*** *the anniversary* • *It was built* ***in order to*** *. . .*

LESSON 2

Take notes from fluent connected speech

GRAMMAR clauses with *whatever, whoever, whenever*

Listening

1a Pair Work Discuss.

1. Which technologies are the people in the photos using? Why do you think they are so popular?
2. Where do you think big companies go to find out how teenagers use technology?
3. How do you think technology development has been influenced by teens and young adults?

b 1.29 Listen.

2a Complete the sentences with information from the listening.

1. Kids drive technology because ____.
2. Kids want technology that can be ____.
3. Text messaging caught on because ____.
4. Facebook developed as ____.
5. Converse sent its market researchers to ____.

b Listen again to check your answers.

Vocabulary | fashions and fads

3a Match the phrases in bold to the definitions.

____ 1. Using teenagers to find out **what's in** and what isn't.
____ 2. They experiment and they automatically **home in on** the new.
____ 3. Anything bigger than a few inches **is out**.
____ 4. Text messaging **caught on** because kids wanted to pass notes to each other during class.
____ 5. All of these things **came about** because of the needs of kids.
____ 6. If you want to **keep up with** the latest style, who do you ask?

a. know the most recent developments
b. focus or direct their attention toward something
c. is fashionable at the moment
d. became popular and fashionable
e. is unfashionable at the moment
f. happened

b Which two phrases in Exercise 3a are exact opposites? Are they formal or informal?

4 Pair Work Discuss.

1. What's the best way to keep up with developments in your profession or hobby?
2. What trends have caught on recently in fashion, music, food, and other areas where you live?
3. How do you think global trends come about? Can you think of any examples?
4. Think of one piece of technology or clothing that used to be "in" but is now "out."

Well, I think the Internet is a great way to keep up with what's happening. I regularly go to several sites related to my profession . . .

Speaking

5 **Group Work** Discuss whether teenagers should be allowed to do the following:

1. watch however much TV they want
2. stay up late whenever they want
3. decorate their room in whatever way they want
4. go wherever they want at night
5. socialize with whomever they want
6. wear whatever they want

Listening

6a ▶1.30 Listen to the conversations. Which questions from Exercise 5 do they discuss?

Conversation 1: ____
Conversation 2: ____
Conversation 3: ____
Conversation 4: ____

b Listen again. What were their opinions?

Grammar | clauses with *whatever, whoever, whenever*

7 Read the Active Grammar box and answer questions a and b at the bottom.

Active Grammar

1. We use *whenever, whatever, whoever*, etc. when it doesn't make any difference *when, what, who*, etc., or when we don't have to be specific. They also mean "we don't know the exact details of *when, what, who*, etc."

   Teenagers shouldn't be allowed to watch however much TV they want. (We don't know how much TV they want to watch.)

   Teenagers should be able to socialize with whomever they want. (We don't know who they want to socialize with.)

2. *What, who, when* are a little different from *whatever, whoever, whenever*. Compare the example sentences below:

   a. *Stop what you are doing now.*
   b. *Stop whatever you are doing now.*
   c. *Whatever you are doing, stop it now.*
   NOT: ~~*What you are doing, stop it now.*~~

3. We often use *however* with an adjective or adverb. It means *No matter how . . .*

   However intelligent you are, eventually you'll meet someone more intelligent.

   However hard he works, he'll never get promoted.

Note: *However* is also a conjunction that means *but* or *on the other hand*.

a. Which sentence(s) in item 2 mean(s), "I know what you are doing and I want you to stop"? _____

b. Which sentence(s) in item 2 mean(s) "I don't care what you are doing, but I want you to stop"? _____

See Reference page 127

8 Complete the sentences with *whenever*, *however*, *whatever*, *whoever*, or *wherever*.

1. ______________ you do, don't lose these keys!
2. Send me an email ______________ you have time.
3. Carry your passport with you ______________ you go.
4. ______________ is at the door, tell them I'm busy.
5. ______________ you travel—by train, car, or bus—the trip will take at least three hours.

9a Complete the second sentence in each pair so that it has the same meaning as the first. Use *whenever*, *however*, *whatever*, *whoever*, or *wherever*.

Ex: If it's the last thing you do, make sure you turn off the power.
Whatever you do, don't forget to turn off the power.

1. Call me if you feel down.
   ________________ down, give me a call.
2. It doesn't matter where we go; they always follow us.
   ________________, they're always close behind.
3. I'll see her as soon as I can.
   ________________, I'll see her.
4. It doesn't matter who we hire; he'll have to be a genius.
   ________________, he'll have to work miracles.
5. Those children can do anything, and it turns out successful.
   ________________ do, they make a success of it.

b 1.31 Listen to check your answers.

10a Complete *The Teenagers' Manifesto* with *whoever*, *whenever*, *whatever*, *however*, and *wherever*.

THE TEENAGERS' MANIFESTO

1. *Allowance—We can spend our allowance on ____________ we like, including clothes, video games, and other things that our parents consider to be a waste of money.*
2. *TV—We can watch ____________ we want on TV, ____________ we want, including late at night.*
3. *Clothes—We can wear ____________ we like.*
4. *Friends—We can go out with ____________ we want.*
5. *Privacy—____________ we want to be alone, we have the right to be in our rooms undisturbed.*
6. *Noise/Music—we can listen to ____________ type of music we choose. If others are trying to work, we will turn down the volume.*
7. *Cell phone use—We can talk to ____________ we wish, ____________ it's necessary.*

b **Pair Work** Would you change anything about *The Teenagers' Manifesto*? If so, what and why?

LESSON 3

Write an autobiographical statement

GRAMMAR logical connectors of time and contrast

CAN DO

Reading

1 **Pair Work** Read the definition of *charisma* below. Then discuss the questions.

> **charisma** /kəˈrɪzmə/ *n* [U] the natural ability to attract and influence other people

1. Who is the most charismatic person you know or know of? In what ways are they charismatic?
2. Is charisma something you can learn, or do you have to be born with it?

Mahatma Gandhi

Madonna

Bill Clinton

Muhammad Ali

Nelson Mandela

Richard Feynman

2 Read the article.

1 According to Joan Collins, Bill Clinton "eats you up with his eyes. I don't know whether it's magic or a trick, but it's the best act I've ever seen." Of course, Bill Clinton and John F. Kennedy had it. Madonna and Muhammad Ali have it, too. It's questionable whether any of the British Royal family have it, although Diana, Princess of Wales, tried to develop it. Charisma. Hard as we try to understand it, the formula remains elusive. All we can do is watch the masters at work and learn from them.

2 Colleen Dawson's grandson was in the same class as Nelson Mandela's grandson. **During** one parents' night, the adults were talking to the teachers. The evening was progressing as usual, **at which point** Mandela suddenly walked in. "Normally we would have asked about homework and other details," says Dawson, "but no one spoke. So he just started talking in a quiet authoritative way about the important job of teaching." **While** the parents and teachers in the room were struck dumb with reverence, **on finding** himself suddenly the center of attention, Mandela found common ground for everyone present—education. Mandela's charisma shone through.

3 Even though charisma is usually associated with politicians, businesspeople, and celebrities, Richard Feynman proved that people in other fields can have it. People **had no sooner begun** a conversation with Feynman than they'd be struck by his love of the subject. Despite the fact that Feynman's field was theoretical physics—not exactly a crowd-pleaser—he had such enthusiasm for the mysteries of the universe that he infected everyone within earshot. The Nobel Prize–winning scientist was a larger-than-life figure and very charismatic. One ex-student recalls, "**He'd hardly have started** a lecture, and you'd notice the whole audience on the edge of their seat."

4 Most of the great leaders in history possessed a star quality that drew others to them and helped them gain power and success. Winston Churchill, Mahatma Gandhi, and Martin Luther King Jr. had a magnetism that is easier to identify with than to explain. Broadcaster and confidence tutor Jeremy Milnes says, "There are some people who are just naturally charismatic, like Johnny Depp, David Bowie, and Marilyn Monroe. But I believe that there are techniques and skills that can be learned and practiced." Milnes says that, much as charisma can be learned, it can't be faked. "Whatever skills and techniques you have are rooted in your own personality." His thoughts are echoed by other experts in the field, who estimate that charisma is 50 percent innate and 50 percent learned.

3 Answer the questions about the reading.

1. Does the writer believe there's a simple way to become charismatic?
2. What did Mandela discuss during parents' night? Why?
3. Does the writer believe charismatic people are associated with particular professions?
4. Why did people want to listen to Feynman?
5. Why does Milnes think there's hope for normal, uncharismatic people?

Grammar | logical connectors of time and contrast

4 Complete the tasks in the Active Grammar box.

Active Grammar

There are many words and phrases used to link ideas in sentences.

Time

1. There are six connectors relating to time **in bold** in the reading. Put them in the correct place in the chart. The first one has been done for you.

It happened soon after another thing.
on finding
It happened at the same time as something else.
It comes at the end of a long, continuous sequence of action. It often introduces a moment of change in the sequence or is the result of this sequence.

Add the following words and phrases to the chart above: when by which time

Contrast

2. There are five expressions of contrast underlined in the reading. Put them in the correct place in the chart.

Expressions that begin a clause (with a subject and a verb).
Expressions that can be followed by a noun phrase or gerund.
Expressions that use adjective/adverb + *as* + subject + verb to emphasize the contrast.

Add the following words and phrases to the chart: in spite of while difficult as it was

See Reference page 127

5 Complete the paragraph using the words and phrases from the box. You will not use all of the phrases.

Oprah Winfrey

despite	hard as	no sooner	even though	when	by which time	much	on getting the job

Until she was six, Oprah Winfrey lived on a farm with her grandmother. ____________ (**1.**) her family's poverty, she had access to books, and she read and preached in church. She got her lucky break ____________, (**2.**) at age 17, she was offered a job at a radio station, ____________ (**3.**) she lacked experience. Her talk show later became *The Oprah Winfrey Show*, which was watched by over 20 million people a day. ____________ (**4.**) as she enjoyed her TV success, Winfrey's real ambition was to act, and in 1985 she starred in *The Color Purple*, for which she received an Oscar nomination. In 1996 she launched Oprah's Book Club. ____________ (**5.**) had it begun than it was a success, influencing the literary choices of millions. In addition, Oprah publishes a magazine: *O, The Oprah Magazine*.

Vocabulary | personal characteristics

6 Match the adjectives on the left to the words or phrases in bold that have the <u>opposite</u> meaning. Check the meaning of any phrases you do not understand.

____ 1. charismatic	a. She **doesn't have much drive or energy.**
____ 2. inspirational	b. He **wavers in the face of problems.**
____ 3. dignified	c. He's very **approachable.** He always has time to talk to people.
____ 4. aloof	d. He's **corrupt.**
____ 5. idealistic	e. She's fairly **nondescript.**
____ 6. tireless	f. She's very **down-to-earth** and practical.
____ 7. trustworthy	g. She's **not very inspiring.**
____ 8. resolute	h. She **lacks *gravitas*.**

7a ▶1.32 Listen to the way the words and expressions above are pronounced. Mark the stresses.

b Listen again. What is the pronunciation of *gn* in *sign*? of *gn* in *dignified*? of *ch* in *much*? of *ch* in *charismatic*?

8 **Pair Work** Discuss.

1. What do you know about the people in the photos? Which adjectives would you use to describe them?
2. Can you think of any other famous people who could be described using the adjectives or the phrases above?

I would say that Hillary Clinton is resolute. For example . . .

Christiane Amanpour

Pelé

Hillary Clinton

Bruce Lee

Writing

9a Read the autobiographical statement in the Writing Bank on page 136 and do the exercises.

b Read the ad below and follow the instructions.

SCHOLARSHIP AWARD – $5,000

Piaget Educational Consultants is offering a scholarship award to study for one year at a university in Australia. The winner will be given lodging, tuition, and $5,000 spending money. Write an autobiographical statement (150–200 words) describing your character and your relationships with colleagues, teachers, and professors. Mention one colleague, teacher, or professor who has influenced you.

Extra Vocabulary Study and Extra Listening Activity in ACTIVEBOOK

Review

1 Add articles to the paragraph where necessary. Change the punctuation accordingly.

The Shanghai World Financial Center

This 1,614-foot (492-meter) high building consists of two elements that correspond to Chinese concept of Earth as square and sky as circle. Hole in top also has practical use—to relieve pressure of wind on building. Glassy Tower is just blocks away from 1,378-foot (420-meter) Jinmao Tower in district of Shanghai that has been designated Asian center for international banking. Tower's lower levels are used for offices, and its upper levels for hotel, art museum, and restaurants.

2 Complete the conversations with *whatever*, *whoever*, *whenever*, *however*, or *wherever*.

1. A: Why do you like Italy?
   B: Because ___________ you go in Italy, you can find amazing architecture.
2. A: What's so different about that school?
   B: There are no required subjects. You can study ___________ you want.
3. A: What time should I come to your house?
   B: Come ___________ you can make it.
4. A: Will you be able to get time off from work?
   B: Yes—they're flexible. I'll talk to ___________ is on duty.
5. A: Will it be faster if we take the bus or the train?
   B: ___________ you travel, it takes over two hours.

3 Choose words from each box to complete the sentences. Change the verb tense where necessary.

come	be	home	catch	keep

in (x2)	up	on (x2)	about	with

1. We ___________ ___________ ___________ the latest developments by reading magazines.
2. I don't think that new type of phone will ever ___________ ___________. It's too ugly.
3. I've lost touch with the music scene. I don't have any idea what ___________ ___________ any more.
4. This extraordinary situation ___________ ___________ because our marketing department had a great idea.
5. Hi-tech companies are increasingly ___________ ___________ ___________ teenagers as their number one consumer.

4 Find and delete any unnecessary words in the text.

An hour with the Body Earth Power Group was enough for me. No sooner but had Carin Brook entered than everyone became silent. Much as I tried to keep my mind open—and despite of the fact that I have been known to do a bit of tree-hugging myself—I couldn't help thinking that this was going to be a waste of time. Brook, even and though she is tiny, had a strong personality. We started stretching in order to "feel the Earth's rhythm," but it didn't last long. I'd hardly but lifted my hands up when she told us all to sit down, close our eyes and "re-visualize ourselves from above." Hard as though I tried, I just couldn't imagine what the top of my head looked like, and in the spite of her promptings to "relax," the hard floor was getting very uncomfortable. Thankfully, 4:00 came, by which the time I was desperate for a nice soft chair and a good meal.

Communication | evaluate personal characteristics

5 **Pair Work** Look at the picture and read the following information about the passengers: One of these people is a spy (a), one is a criminal (b), one used to be famous (c), one will be famous (d), one is a doctor (e), one is a lawyer (f), one has a dark secret (g), one is a journalist (h), and one is a soldier (i). Who is who? Guess the identity of the people and label the picture.

6 Imagine you are one of the people. Complete the short profile below.

My name is ______________
I work as a ______________
I am ______________
I believe in ______________
My strengths are ______________
____
My weaknesses are ______________
____
I will always ______________
____

7 Imagine that the plane crashes. Everyone survives, and you all find yourselves on a desert island. You decide to start a new community. Your character wants to be the leader. Think about the following questions.

1. What are your ideas for leading the community?
2. How will you persuade the others that you should be in charge?
3. What experiences do you have that will be useful?

8a **Group Work** Present your ideas and argue your case for becoming the leader of the new community.

b Elect a leader and explain your choice to other groups.

UNIT 7
The natural world

A

B

C

D

Warm Up

1 **Pair Work** Discuss. Where are the animals in the photos? Which are being used by people? How? Do you approve of the way they are being used? Why or why not?

2 **Pair Work** Discuss.

1. Name two or more animals for each category:

mammal	endangered species
reptile	exotic animal
carnivore	predator

2. Name two or more animals that live in the following places:

in a sanctuary or nature preserve
in the wild
in a cage

3. What do you know about the following issues?

the fur trade	animal testing
animal rights	over-hunting and over-fishing

Explain procedures

GRAMMAR adjective clauses

Reading

1 Look at the two titles in the reading. What do you think the article will be about? Read and check your prediction.

How watching animals will save us

Becoming better observers of animal behavior may be the key to surviving natural disasters in the future. During the tsunami disaster of 2004, over 300,000 people died. No one has counted the number of animals killed, but we know that it wasn't many. All over the region, before the disaster struck, animals were behaving strangely.

Shortly before the tsunami, in Khaolak, Thailand, 12 elephants that were giving tourists rides became agitated. They suddenly left their usual habitat, carrying four surprised Japanese tourists to safety. On the eastern coast of India, flamingos, which should have been breeding at that time of year, suddenly flew to higher ground. Of the 2,000 wild pigs that inhabit an Indian nature reserve, only one was found dead after the tsunami.

The idea that animals are able to predict disasters is nothing new. In fact, it has been well documented over the years. Twelve hours before Hurricane Charlie hit Florida in 2004, 14 electronically tagged sharks left their natural habitat and stayed in deeper waters for two weeks. The sharks, which were being observed by US biologists, had never done that before. They escaped the hurricane. In the winter of 1975 in Haicheng, China, snakes that would normally have been hibernating were seen on the ground. Days later, there was an earthquake that measured 7.3 on the Richter Scale.

Unlike human beings, wild animals perceive a great deal of information about the world around them. Their senses are sharper, and they can feel even the smallest changes in the environment. In other words, they see natural warnings that are invisible to the human eye. Ancient people probably had similar "animal instincts," which they needed to survive but which have been lost to us as modern technology leads us further away from the dangers that nature poses.

The real question is, can we use the reactions of animals to save ourselves from natural disasters? Animal behavior expert Rupesh Kaneira believes we have no choice. "The technology that we rely on isn't always perfect, and in poorer countries it isn't even available. Animals know the environment better than any of us. When they run for their lives, we must follow."

And how rats will rescue us . . .

In the earthquake capitals of the world—Japan, Los Angeles, Turkey—rats will soon be man's new best friend.

In the aftermath of an earthquake, rescue teams send in dogs that are trained to smell people. No one knows how many lives they have saved, but there are, of course, drawbacks: dogs are big, and they can't get into small spaces. Now a new research project is using a smaller animal to save lives: the rat.

How does it work? First, the rat is trained to smell people. When it does, the rat's brain gives off a signal, similar to what happens when a dog smells a bomb. The trained rats are sent into the wreckage. On their back is a very small radio, which is connected to the rat's brain. The rescuers, at a safe distance, monitor the radio signals. When the rat's brain activity jumps, the rescuers know that someone is alive.

Of course, there are already robots that can do this job, one of which looks and moves like a snake, but rats are better because they can smell more efficiently than robots, whose noses don't work well when there are other smells around. Rats also crawl efficiently in destroyed buildings—something that robots are not as good at—and they don't need electricity. What's more, rats have a survival instinct: they get out when it isn't safe.

2 Answer the questions.

1. What did the animals do before the natural disasters occurred?
2. How do we know what the sharks did before Hurricane Charlie?
3. What specific ability allows animals to "predict" natural disasters?
4. How do rescue teams know that a rescue rat has found someone?

3 **Pair Work** Discuss.

1. What differences between humans and animals does the article describe?
2. Do you believe in a "sixth sense" or "animal instincts"?
3. Do you think these ideas for using animals will be successful? What problems might there be?

Grammar | adjective clauses

4 Read the sentences from the reading in the Active Grammar box and underline the adjective clauses. Then answer the questions.

Active Grammar

Restrictive adjective clauses	Non-restrictive adjective clauses
Twelve elephants that were giving tourists rides became agitated.	*Flamingos, which should have been breeding at that time of year, suddenly flew to higher ground.*
Of the 2,000 wild pigs that inhabit an Indian nature reserve, only one was found dead.	*The sharks, which were being observed by US biologists, had never done that before.*
There are already robots that can do this job.	*Rats are better because they can smell more efficiently than robots, whose noses don't work well.*
The technology that we rely on isn't always perfect.	

1. Which clauses identify a person or thing and cannot be deleted without changing the meaning of the sentence?
2. Which clauses add extra information and can be deleted without changing the meaning of the sentence?

See Reference page 128

5 Answer the questions.

1. In which type of adjective clause (restrictive or non-restrictive) can we use *that* instead of *who* or *which*?
2. When do we use commas with adjective clauses?
3. Which clause ends with a preposition? Find another example in the final paragraph of the reading and underline it. Where does the preposition go in formal English?
4. Find the sentence in the final paragraph of the reading that contains the structure *one of which*.

6 **Pair Work** Do the pairs of sentences have the same meaning? If not, how are they different? Which sentences are incorrect?

1. a. Monkeys whose DNA is similar to that of humans are often used in research into the brain.
   b. Monkeys, whose DNA is similar to that of humans, are often used in research into the brain.
2. a. Guide dogs were first used by soldiers who had been blinded during World War One.
   b. Guide dogs were first used by soldiers, who had been blinded during World War One.
3. a. The funnel spider's web, which is extremely fine, was used to cover wounds.
   b. The funnel spider's web, that is extremely fine, was used to cover wounds.
4. a. Homing pigeons are able to return, weeks later, to the place which they came from.
   b. Homing pigeons are able to return, weeks later, to the place from which they came.

7a Rewrite the questions, including the phrases in the box. Add commas where necessary.

1. Should hunting be allowed?
2. Should zoos be banned?
3. Should the Amazon rainforest be protected? If so, how?
4. Should the use of fur for clothing be banned?

- that take animals from their natural habitat
- that is done only for sport and not for food
- about which there has been much debate in the fashion industry
- which is being destroyed

b **Pair Work** Discuss the questions. Think of arguments for both sides of each issue.

Listening

8 ▶2.02 Listen. Mark the sentences true (*T*), false (*F*), or doesn't say (*?*). Then listen again to check answers.

____ 1. You need to do some planning before you buy your rabbits.
____ 2. Rabbits eat almost any type of food.
____ 3. You should be vaccinated.
____ 4. You should have at least two rabbits in a hutch.
____ 5. Lots of people choose a dog because it looks cute.
____ 6. The speaker thinks it's a bad idea to keep a dog outside.
____ 7. The owner's lifestyle is an important consideration in choosing the breed of dog.
____ 8. The speaker knows a lot of dog-owners.

Pronunciation | unstressed prepositions

9a How is *to* pronounced in these phrases and sentences from the listening?

1. The first thing you need to do . . .
2. You just need to do a little planning.
3. You have to make sure to get food that they like.
4. You have to clean out the hutch once a week or more . . .

b ▶2.03 Listen to check.

c ▶2.04 Identify the unstressed prepositions in the following sentences. How are they pronounced? Listen and check.

1. A lot of people, for example, just go for the cutest dog they can find.
2. The first thing you need to do is ask yourself a few questions.
3. . . . the next thing to think about is what type of dog would be best for you.
4. . . . if you spend most of your time at home watching TV, get a less active dog.

10 **Pair Work** Think of something that you know how to do well. Make notes on the steps involved. Then tell your partner how to get started. Use some of the language from the How To box.

Learning how to windsurf is hard at first, but it's worth the trouble. The first thing you should do is find a good teacher. You'll probably need to rent the equipment at first . . .

How To:

Explain procedures

Prefacing with a general statement	• *It can be a little tricky at first.* • *It's pretty straightforward.* • *It's really easy./It's a piece of cake.*
Sequencing	• *First . . ./The first thing you have to do is . . .* • *Then/Second/The next step is to . . .* • *Finally,*
Checking understanding	• *OK?/Got it?/Any questions?*

Writing

11 A friend is going to stay in your home while you are away. Write three notes explaining how to use your washing machine, feed your pet, water your plants, etc.

LESSON 2

Make inferences based on extended prose

GRAMMAR verbs followed by infinitives or gerunds: meaning

CAN DO

Speaking

1 **Pair Work** Discuss. What's the hottest place you have been to? What problems could you have visiting a very hot place? Think about things such as animals, places to stay, health.

Listening

2a ▶2.05 Listen to the first part of David Clark's story. Answer the questions.

1. What does David need from the bureaucrat?
2. What is the bureaucrat's attitude toward David's trip? How do we know?
3. The bureaucrat has a sense of humor. What does he say that shows this?

b **Pair Work** Discuss. What do you think the journey will be like? What do you think the Danakil Depression looks like? How do you think David will feel when he arrives?

I don't think David knows what he's getting into. I bet he is going to be surprised . . .

c ▶2.06 Listen to the second part of the story. Were your predictions correct?

3 **Group Work** Discuss.

1. Why do you think David wanted to make this journey?
2. Why do you think explorers go to extreme places?
3. Why do you think David is disappointed with the Danakil Depression?
4. Would you like to go there? Why or why not?
5. "It is better to travel than to arrive." Do you agree with this proverb?

Vocabulary | descriptive language

4a Listen to the story on page 83 again. Match the words and phrases on the left with the words on the right to make common collocations.

____ 1. spectacular	a. level
____ 2. permanent	b. town
____ 3. tourist	c. settlement
____ 4. below sea	d. landscape
____ 5. active	e. volcano
____ 6. ghost	f. site

b Which of the collocations could be used to describe the photos below?

1

2

3

5 Complete the sentences with collocations from Exercise 4a.

1. The world's most popular ______________ is the area around the Eiffel Tower, in Paris.
2. Mount Etna in Sicily, Italy, is the world's most ______________.
3. Antarctica is the only continent on which there is no ______________. It is too cold!
4. The Dead Sea is the lowest point on Earth. It is 1,371 feet (418 meters) ______________.
5. Walhalla, Australia, is a rare example of a ______________ that came back to life. Originally a gold mining town, it was abandoned when the gold ran out, but is now popular with tourists.
6. Some of the world's most ______________ can be found in Cappadocia, Turkey.

6a Read Audioscripts 2.05 and 2.06 on page 140. What things and people do the words in the box describe? Look up the definitions of any words that you don't know.

Ex: *"Drone" describes the noise of a fan.*

Verbs	Adjectives
drone	warped
zig-zag	vibrant
loom	hunched
trespass	drenched
	parched

b **Pair Work** Now think of other things you can describe using the adjectives.

Vibrant—the colors were vibrant

Barcelona has a vibrant nightlife. She has a vibrant personality.

Grammar | verbs followed by infinitives or gerunds: meaning

7 Complete the tasks in the Active Grammar box.

Active Grammar

Some verbs can be followed by an infinitive or a gerund. Sometimes the meaning changes. Compare the sentences and answer the questions.

Mean

1. Which verb phrase means a) intended, b) involves?

   ___ *Going to the Danakil Depression **means walking** into hell on Earth.*

   ___ *David **meant to write** a book after his trips.*

Remember

2. Which verb phrase describes a) a responsibility or something that you need to do, b) a memory of the past?

   ___ *He **remembers experiencing** a feeling of emptiness when he arrived.*

   ___ *They tell you . . . to **remember to drink** even when you're not thirsty.*

Regret

3. Which verb phrase means a) a feeling of sadness about something in the past, b) a formal apology?

   ___ *I **regret to inform you** that your application for a visa has been turned down.*

   ___ *I didn't **regret going** to the Danakil Depression.*

Stop

4. Which verb phrase means a) paused in order to do something, b) completely finished something?

   ___ *We **stopped to visit** a ghost town.*

   ___ *David **stopped looking** for vegetation and wildlife once he realized nothing survived in the Danakil Depression.*

Try

5. Which verb phrase describes a) an experiment to see what will happen (as a solution to a problem), b) an effort to do something difficult?

   ___ *They had **tried to build** a railway.*

   ___ *He **tried drinking** more water but he still felt terrible.*

Go on

6. Which verb phrase means a) continued an action, b) did something after finishing something else?

   ___ *They waved and **went on riding**.*

   ___ *David Clark **went on to write** a book about his experiences.*

See Reference page 128

8 Using patterns from the Active Grammar box, add two words to complete each sentence.

Ex: I don't remember *taking the* photo, but it turned out really well.

1. After six hours of driving, we take a break by the roadside.
2. We visit the cathedral, but it was closed that day.
3. Even after I told her to be quiet, she went loudly.
4. She regrets so early this morning. Now she's really tired.
5. I remembered traveler's checks this time. Last time, I forgot and lost all my money.
6. After leaving school with a law degree, she to become a famous lawyer.

Speaking

9a Circle the correct choice.

1. For me, a vacation means _to lie/lying_ on a beach.
2. I try _spending/to spend_ time outside whenever I can.
3. I'll never stop _traveling/to travel_, even when I'm old.
4. I've never regretted _to go/going_ anywhere.

b **Pair Work** Are the sentences true or false for you? Expand on your answer.

I prefer doing something active when I'm on vacation, like hiking or skiing. . .

LESSON 3

Write an ad for an object

GRAMMAR *as . . . as*; describing quantity

Listening

1a **Pair Work** Can you think of any jobs that involve animals? What skills do you think are required?

b 2.07 Listen and discuss the questions. What are Sharon's job responsibilities? How does Sharon feel about her job? What qualities do you think are necessary for a job like this? Would you like Sharon's job? Why or why not?

Reading

2 Read the article and then circle the correct choice to complete each statement.

ANIMALS ONLINE

1 Can you really buy anything on the Internet? Believe it or not, some of the items marketed on the Internet as gifts for children or as prestige items for the home are actually live animals, many of them endangered species.

2 Despite international laws against the sale of endangered species, animals such as gorillas, tigers, chimpanzees, and leopard cubs are bought and sold on the Internet, some for as little as a few hundred dollars. According to a report by the IFAW (the International Fund for Animal Welfare), well over 1,400 live, exotic animals were being sold online in just one 6-week period. "That's an astonishing number," says one IFAW employee involved in the study. Of these 1,400 animals, most of the online ads were for birds, though in the US alone, 13 primates, 5 big cats, and 2 rhinos were for sale.

3 So what exactly would it cost, and what would you have to do to buy a wild animal? The researchers found chimpanzees dressed as dolls for $60,000 each. What about proof that you can look after and house an animal adequately? None needed. Although gorillas require space and very specialized care, the researchers also found a gorilla for sale for $8,100. For those with a little more head room, giraffes can also be bought. Got-PetsOnline.com offered a young giraffe for $15,000.

4 Though the vast majority of animals for sale are birds, monkeys make up a large portion of Internet sales, and experts are particularly concerned by the way they are marketed and traded on the Internet. A number of websites describe them as if they are little more than large, hairy dolls. They offer "accessories, such as diapers, bottles, and clothes." The traders even have a cute name for themselves: "monkey moms." They call the animals themselves "monkids." Virtually none of these websites explains how to take care of the animals.

5 When the IFAW undercover investigators contacted some of the US traders, they were told that it would be possible to export them to European countries—a blatant breach of EU law. There is also concern that demand for monkeys and chimps is fueling the illegal trapping and trading of wild species. Although there were approximately 2 million chimpanzees in the wild a century ago, there are as few as 150,000 left, and one research project says that by 2020 there will be a maximum of 100,000.

6 The effort to stamp out the live animal trade is made more difficult by the number of websites involved and by the fact that it is sometimes almost impossible to track sales made offline once sellers and buyers have made initial contact on the Internet. The IFAW's message to online shoppers is straightforward: "Buying wildlife online is as damaging as killing it yourself."

1. The animals are marketed as if they are _useful around the home/dangerous/toys_.
2. The IFAW was surprised _at the size of the illegal market for wild animals/to find endangered species for sale/at the way the traders treat the animals_.
3. The online animal trade is one cause of _economic problems in poor countries/violent crime/illegal hunting_.

3 **Pair Work** Discuss.

1. Should people have wild animals as pets? Give reasons.
2. What can be done to stop the illegal trade? Is it possible to stop illegal Internet sales in general?

Grammar | *as . . . as*; describing quantity

4 Complete the tasks in the Active Grammar box.

Active Grammar

1. *as* + adjective + *as* is used to:
   - show that two things are equal
   - describe quantity

   Find three examples in the article (paragraphs 2, 5, and 6). Which meanings does *as* + adjective + *as* have in these cases?

2. There are other phrases commonly used to describe quantity. Look at the phrases below and find their opposites in the article.

paragraph
- 2 *as much as* → ______________
- 2 *well under* → ______________
- 4 *a tiny minority of* → ______________
- 4 *virtually all (of)* → ______________
- 5 *precisely* → ______________
- 5 *as many as* → ______________
- 5 *a minimum of* → ______________

a. Which phrases use numbers? (*For example,* ***as much as 20***)

b. Which two phrases can't be used with count nouns?

See Reference page 128

Pronunciation

5a ▶2.08 Listen to how *as* is pronounced in the sentences.

b **Pair Work** Now create sentences with some of the phrases from the Active Grammar box. Practice saying them.

The vast majority of my friends have pets.

6 Put the words in order. Begin and end each sentence with the underlined words.

1. Hamsters many birth to as offspring can as give eight at a time.
2. The to able majority domestic repeat of parrots are vast human speech.
3. The life as housefly of 17 is short as a days.
4. Koalas lives their virtually of spend all asleep: 22 hours per day.
5. Tortoises years, well longer a over 100 live deal can great than humans.

Speaking

7 **Pair Work** Discuss.

1. Do you own or have you ever owned a pet? What type of animal?
2. Would you ever consider buying an animal on the Internet? In what circumstances?

I might consider buying a common pet online. I'd still prefer to "meet" it in person, though.

Vocabulary | buying and selling

8a Match each phrase on the left with an expression with a similar meaning on the right.

____ 1. It's in excellent condition.	a.	It's one of a kind.
____ 2. It's the latest model.	b.	It's used.
____ 3. It's second hand.	c.	It's on the market.
____ 4. It's available now.	d.	It's not in perfect condition (it's been used a lot).
____ 5. It's handcrafted.	e.	You can choose from a selection of . . .
____ 6. It's brand new.	f.	It's made by hand.
____ 7. It features . . .	g.	It's still in its packaging.
____ 8. It has some wear and tear.	h.	It's as good as new.
____ 9. It's unique.	i.	It includes . . .
____ 10. It comes in a wide range of . . .	j.	It's state of the art.

b **Pair Work** Say a sentence using a phrase from the Vocabulary. Without looking at the book, your partner rephrases the sentence, using his or her own words. Take turns creating and rephrasing more sentences.

Speaking

9 **Pair Work** Which phrases from the Vocabulary could you use to describe the things in the photos? Were any animals used to make these things?

Writing

10a Read the ads on an Internet auction site. Find five spelling mistakes and five preposition mistakes.

b Choose something that you would like to sell (for example—furniture, books, toys, clothes) and write an ad describing the object, price, condition, etc.

c **Group Work** Show your ads to each other. Ask and answer questions about the different items, and try to find something you would like to buy.

d Tell the class about the item you decided to buy and explain why you chose it.

http://www.sellit.com

Sellit.com *the **BEST** auction site!*

Animal Instincts by well-known psychologist Paul Marrow. The book is slitely damaged on the spine and has a few highlighted passages in the first chapter, but otherwise on excellent condition.	bids (0)
Children's T-shirt and shorts combo, feeturing *Animal Magic* design. You can chose for red, green, or blue. All are brand new and hand designed. *Animal Magic* hats also availlable.	bids (2)
Dog kennel for sale. Some wear and tare on the door. Made by hand in Mumbai, this is one in a kind.	bids (3)
State in the art fish tank. 1 yard long, 24 inches wide, 30 inches deep. Includes large oxygen tube and plants. Bought just two weeks ago, it's as good of new.	bids (11)

Extra Vocabulary Study and Extra Listening Activity in *ACTIVEBOOK*

Review

1 Complete the paragraphs by inserting the phrases in the box in the correct places.

that trains	when they	that will
who spend	who work	that has
who trained		

One problem that faces many prison inmates, most of their time locked up, is how to develop self-esteem and do something useful. One idea been piloted at a prison in Washington is to get the inmates to train dogs eventually help disabled people. The project has been a great success. The relationship between the inmates and the guards at the prison has improved considerably. Many of the inmates, leave the prison, go on to work with animals.

In another scheme, Pilot Dogs, a company dogs for the blind in Ohio put five dogs in the hands of prison inmates, the dogs successfully.

2 Combine the two sentences into one sentence, using adjective clauses.

Ex: The animals escaped to higher ground. The animals sensed the tsunami approaching.
The animals, which sensed the tsunami approaching, escaped to higher ground.

1. I got a new dog at the animal shelter. The shelter rescues homeless animals.
2. Rats can smell more efficiently than robots. The rats are sent into damaged buildings.
3. The explorer was amazed by the view. She had hiked for hours up the mountain.
4. The volcano erupted last night. The volcano hadn't been active for years.
5. Many animals are sold illegally. The animals are sold on the Internet.
6. Zoos can help save endangered species. The species might otherwise become extinct.

3 Circle the correct choice to complete each sentence.

1. I meant *to say/saying* something to you earlier, but now I've forgotten what it was.
2. She's such a crazy dresser. I hate *to think/thinking* what she's wearing tonight!
3. He remembered *to lock/locking* the door this time. Last time, we got robbed!
4. We regret *to tell/telling* you that your application was turned down.
5. Please stop *to talk/talking*. I can't hear the movie.
6. She tried *to drink/drinking* warm milk before bedtime, but she still couldn't sleep.
7. Despite a difficult childhood, he went on *to become/becoming* the world's greatest athlete.

4 Use the words in the box to complete the sentences.

maximum	none	well
virtually	vast	as
approximately	much	

1. Apparently you can buy a leopard for ____________ little as $10,000 on the Internet.
2. A ____________ majority of the public—nearly 90 percent—voted to keep the old currency.
3. There are ____________ 6,000 in the hall, but we don't know the exact number.
4. I spent ____________ all my money on the entrance fee. I only have $5 left for food.
5. This elevator holds a ____________ of eight people.
6. He's huge! He must be ____________ over 6 feet tall.
7. You can earn as ____________ as $200,000 a year, if you work hard enough.
8. Virtually ____________ of the team members had ever played there before.

Communication | reach a compromise on a plan

Paradise Island has 31 square miles (50 square kilometers) of land that can be developed.
The land has some hilly areas and a little forest.
The land and climate are good for growing vegetables, fruit, etc.
There is a lot of wildlife on the island.
There are two natural springs on the island. The spring water is very good for people's health.
The island nearby has recently become more popular with tourists.

5 Look at the photo and read the notes about Paradise Island.

6 **Pair Work** Make a list of all the things you could do with the island if it belonged to you. Compare your ideas with other students.

7 ▶2.09 Listen to the discussion. Are any of their ideas the same as or similar to yours?

8 **SPEAKING EXCHANGE** Work in groups. Student A: read the role on page 132. Student B: read the role on page 135. Student C: read the role on page 133. Then discuss what to do with the land. You must agree to do something with it; if you can't agree on one thing, you can combine some of your ideas.

9 Report back to the class. What did you decide to do with the land?

UNIT 8
Problems and issues

A

B

C

D

Warm Up

1 **Pair Work** Discuss. What is happening in the photos? What issues are represented? Do you think they are important? Why or why not?

2 Which photos can be associated with the words and phrases in the box?

giant corporations	global warming	identity theft	cloning	oil spill
cost and safety issues	multiculturalism	pollution	energy	

3 **Group Work** Discuss.

1. What issues have been in the news recently? Do any of them affect you personally? Which issues do you think are the most important?
2. Which issues do you think will become more important in the future? Why?

LESSON 1 Stall for time when asked a difficult question

GRAMMAR reporting verbs

CAN DO

Speaking

1a Match each photo to *two* sentences below.

____ 1. **It's a waste of space.** Most of it is either reruns or ads, and it ruins your eyes.

____ 2. **It's overrated.** You can't trust the information on it, because anyone can publish things on it.

____ 3. **They've been disastrous for humanity.** If they're poisonous for insects, they're poisonous for humans.

____ 4. **We can do without them.** No one really needs to have a conversation every five minutes.

____ 5. **It's underrated.** It lets us find information quickly and keep in touch with people.

____ 6. **We can't do without them.** They're essential for talking to people no matter where you are.

____ 7. **It's indispensable.** It gives us up-to-date news, movies, and many other kinds of programs.

____ 8. **They've had big benefits for humanity.** They make it possible to grow more food with less work.

b **Pair Work** Discuss your opinions on the issues in Exercise 1a.

I agree that pesticides are bad for our health. On the other hand, . . .

Reading

2 **Pair Work** Discuss. What do you think are some of the most important problems facing the world today? Can you think of any possible inventions that can solve them?

3 Read the article.

FUTURE INVENTIONS

The editors of* Future World Magazine *look at the inventions we will need for a brighter future.

1 Everyone has their favorite invention. Some of us even make lists of them. One survey recently named the toilet as the greatest invention ever. Another survey named the bicycle, which received twice as many votes as the World Wide Web. That's the past, but what about the future? What inventions will shape our lives? J.B.S. Haldane, a scientist, once made his prediction for the future. He said that whatever hadn't happened would happen and no one would be safe from it. Whether you agree or not, one thing is beyond doubt: human beings need to invent a few things pretty quickly. Here is our own list:

2 Number one is a new source of power. Oil is running out. A teenager, in a recent letter to a newspaper, wrote that it would take over a hundred years to produce fresh oil. He was wrong by a few million years. Once our oil is gone, it's gone forever. We have about fifty years' worth left, less if rates of industrialization accelerate. A hundred million new cars will need a lot of oil. At a recent conference about the world's future, scientist Hilary Craft said we had already found the answer: solar power. She believes that we will eventually have enormous mirrors in the sky that will provide the world's electricity.

3 Number two on our list is a plan to deal with waste. Many societies bury their waste underground or dump it into the sea. Now we're running out of space. If we want to avoid choking the Earth, we'd better find a way to recycle more effectively. According to inventor Ray Kurzweill, tiny self-replicating microscopic robots will convert trash into new sources of energy. Another inventor, Clara Petrovic, said she was working on a prototype that would convert waste into bricks and other building material.

4 Number three on our list is biological ID. Criminal investigator Alexis Smithson said that in the past, thieves had always taken objects. Now they steal identities. ID theft is the fastest-growing type of crime. So how will we stop it? You can expect to have tiny microchips injected into your body; scanners will read your genetic

continued on page 93

information to check your ID. Or worse, you may need to provide skin cells whenever you go shopping. Imagine scratching yourself in the checkout line every time you buy the groceries. Supermarkets will never be the same.

Finally, medicine. In the past, a cold could kill you. Now we are examining people's genes for signs of future illness. Find the disease early enough, and you can prevent it. Glen Hiemstra of Futurist.com recently claimed that somewhere on planet Earth there is a young child who will be the first person to live forever. If that happens, we'll need another invention: a new retirement system.

4 Circle the correct choice to complete each sentence.

1. The writers of the article ____.
   a. think that the bicycle is the greatest invention
   b. are interested in things that haven't been invented yet
2. Two inventors are trying to find ways to ____.
   a. use our trash productively
   b. reduce waste
3. Protection against ID theft will involve ____.
   a. microchips in every object we own
   b. technology "reading" the human body
4. According to the article, the main invention in medicine will be ____.
   a. a way to predict the illnesses a person is vulnerable to
   b. a pill that will enable people to live forever

Grammar | reporting verbs

5 Find one example of reported speech in each paragraph of the text. What happens to verb tenses when we report speech? Which example from the text doesn't shift the tenses back?

6 Read the rules and complete the task in the Active Grammar box.

Active Grammar

Often we use a reporting verb to *paraphrase* the meaning:

"Let's go home." → *She **thinks** we should leave.*

"Why don't we discuss it with everyone?" → *He **suggested** that we talk about it with everyone.*

"It was my mistake." → *He **admitted** that it was his fault.*

Match reporting verbs with similar meanings. Are there any differences in meaning or formality?

	A	B
____	1. admit	a. maintain
____	2. remember	b. imply
____	3. tell	c. respond
____	4. answer	d. confess
____	5. suggest	e. recollect
____	6. threaten	f. inform
____	7. insist	g. warn

See Reference page 129

7 Cross out the incorrect choice in each sentence.

1. I *warned/informed/threatened* them that ID theft was common.
2. He *suggested that they discuss/suggested discussing/implied discussing* immigration at the meeting.
3. She *insisted/maintained/informed* that technology would solve the problem.
4. He *admitted/told/confessed* that he knew nothing about developments in biotechnology.
5. We must *tell/inform/suggest* the audience about the research into global warming.

8 **Pair Work** Report the conversation using the verbs from the box.

admit	suggest	remember
warn	confess	

Mike: I never recycle anything, because I'm too lazy.
Mike admitted that he never recycles anything because he's too lazy.
Sarah: If we don't start recycling, the consequences will be serious for the planet.
David: So why don't we start a recycling group in the community?
Sarah: Wait a minute. There already is one.
Mike: Well, there was. I started one, but then it became too much work, so we stopped.

Listening

9 Look at the pictures. Can you guess what these new inventions do?

10 2.10 Listen to seven people answering the question: "Which new invention would you most like to see?" Write the number of the speaker next to the pictures.

a.
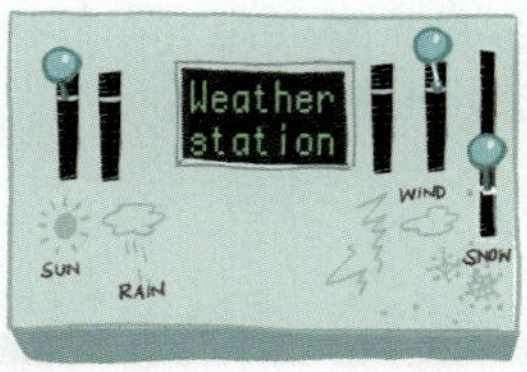

b.

c.
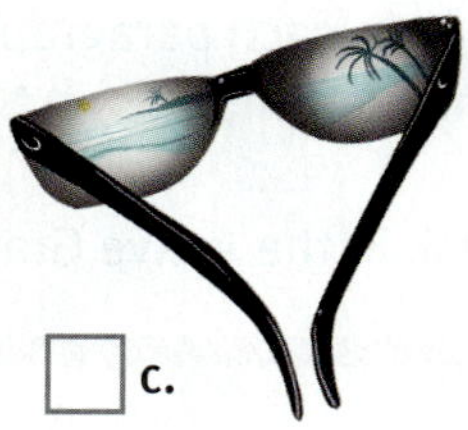

d.

e.
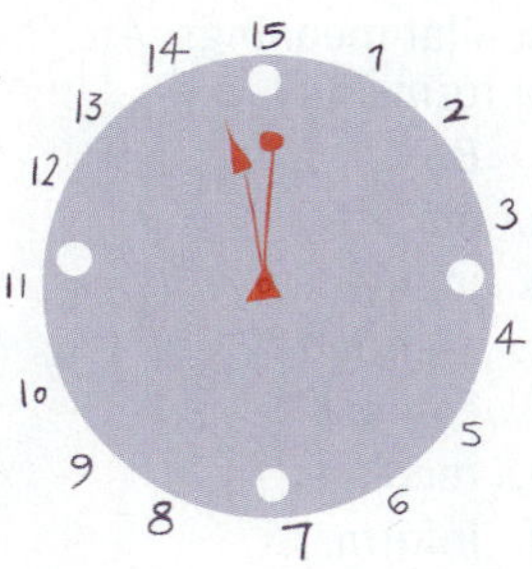

f.

g.
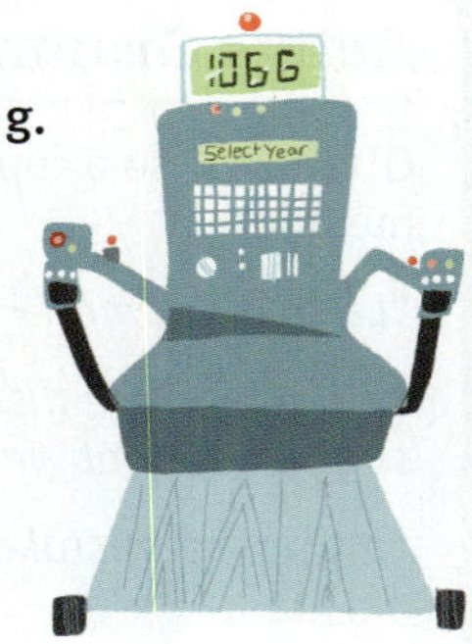

11a **Pair Work** Discuss. Try to use the expressions from the How To box.

1. Which inventions in Exercise 10 do you think are a good idea? Why?
2. What other invention(s) do you think might help the world?
3. What other invention(s) do you think might help you at work or at home?
4. What invention could you not do without?
5. Are there any modern inventions that you think are overrated?

How To:

Stall for time (when you're asked a difficult question)

That's a good question.	*Let me see.*
That's tricky.	*I'll have to think about that.*
That's a difficult question.	*Well, . . .*

b Work with another partner. Report your original partner's opinions.

Tara told me that she would like to have a robot to do the housework. She also . . .

Discuss lifestyle

GRAMMAR continuous forms

Listening

1 **Pair Work** Look at the photos. What types of people do you think Thomas and Elise are?

Thomas

2 2.11 Listen to Thomas and Elise. How do their opinions and lifestyles differ?

3a Choose the best answer.

1. What made Thomas change his lifestyle?
   a. He received an important email.
   b. He couldn't enjoy Rome because he was obsessed with work.
   c. He went to the beach and fell in love with the sea.
2. Why does he think people carry technology around with them?
   a. Because they wish they were in the office.
   b. Because it helps them feel less stressed.
   c. Because they are worried they will miss important pieces of information.
3. What has Thomas learned from living near the ocean?
   a. That human actions and money aren't so important.
   b. That you can't make much money there.
   c. That he should have left his city job much earlier.
4. What do Elise's friends think of her working life?
   a. They think it's making her sick.
   b. They think she's too competitive.
   c. They think Elise never has enough time.
5. Why does Elise carry around so much technology?
   a. Because she doesn't have an office.
   b. Because she travels a lot and doesn't want an office.
   c. Because she travels a lot, and the technology gives her confidence.

Elise

b Listen again to check your answers.

Vocabulary | lifestyles

4 Listen again and read the Audioscript on page 141. Match the expressions with the correct definitions.

____ 1. tearing my hair out	a. the excitement
____ 2. the be-all and end-all	b. be too exhausted to continue a long-term action (usually a job)
____ 3. security blanket	c. something that makes you feel safe and confident
____ 4. burn out	d. the most important thing
____ 5. the buzz	e. getting into a panic because of frustration

5 **Pair Work** Discuss.

1. Do you agree that "the world is one stressed-out place"? What are the main causes of this stress?
2. What do you think are the symptoms of "running out of time syndrome"? Do you—or does anyone you know—suffer from these?

I agree that many people are stressed. Some of the causes of stress are technology . . .

Grammar | continuous forms

6 Look at the sentences from the listening on page 95. Match each sentence to the correct continuous form.

____ 1. I'd been having dinner with a client all evening.
____ 2. I was tearing my hair out trying to get access to a computer.
____ 3. The waves will be rolling in every morning long after we're gone.
____ 4. I've been working at an investment company for about four years.
____ 5. In fact, the statistics are getting worse – I think it's under three years now.

a. present continuous
b. past continuous
c. present perfect continuous
d. past perfect continuous
e. future continuous

7 Complete the tasks after each rule in the Active Grammar box.

Active Grammar

1. We can use continuous tenses to describe activities. Match the sentences from Exercise 6 to the uses below.
   a. Actions that are background events (possibly finished) before another event (*sentences 1 and ____*).
   b. Actions that are temporary or incomplete, or we want to stress the duration (usually a long time) (*sentence ____*).
   c. Actions that are repeated (*sentence ____*).
   d. Actions that are in the process of changing (*sentence ____*).
2. The continuous forms (especially the past continuous) can also be used to sound more tentative and less direct in suggestions, offers, and inquiries.
   I was wondering if . . . ?
   Can you think of any examples?
3. Stative verbs are usually not used in the continuous. Write four more common stative verbs for each category below.

Verbs of personal feeling:
like
Verbs of thought:
know
Verbs of the senses:
appear

See Reference page 129

8a Rewrite the sentences using a continuous form of the verb. How does the meaning change?

1. I've read that book.
2. I'll work until about 8:00 tonight.
3. She hit me.
4. The first chapter is written.
5. What music do you listen to?
6. He had lost his hair.
7. We go to work at 8:00.

b Write responses to the sentences in Exercise 8a—both the original sentences and your sentences in the continuous.

Ex: I've read that book. *Was it good?*
I'm reading that book. *Are you enjoying it?*

9 Use the verbs in the box to complete the paragraphs below. Change the verb tense where necessary. Use the continuous if possible.

urge	go back	grow	begin	drive	seem	advocate	question	quote

At the beginning of last month I looked out of my window and saw the telltale signs: increased traffic, early-morning crowds, glum faces. Yes, that's right, the children ________________ (**1.**) to school and parents ________________ (**2.**) a new work year. And I asked myself an old question: do we have the work/life balance right?

A new generation of economists ________________ (**3.**) the century-long assumption of economics: that men and women are motivated by more—more profit, more possessions, more work. Is a hectic pace of life what we really want? And will it make us happy?

The number of people in mid-career who ________________ (**4.**) ready to abandon the desperate climb up the corporate ladder ________________ (**5.**). And now, several journalists and social commentators ________________ (**6.**) us to go slower and enjoy life.

Tom Hodgkinson, in *How to Be Idle*, says that prominent literary figures ________________ (**7.**) the idle life for centuries. He ________________ (**8.**) Bertrand Russell, Samuel Johnson and others. Carl Honoré's *In Praise of Slow* also suggests that slowing down may be the best way, and he provides a telling anecdote. He recalls a time recently when he ________________ (**9.**) extremely fast in Italy because he was late for a Slow Food meal. The irony of it!

Speaking

10 Read the profile of Dana Kolansky. Would you say she has a busy life?

Profile of Dana Kolansky

- Dana is a store clerk and part-time anthropology student.
- Before getting a job as a store clerk, she had been working in a bar.
- After finishing work she usually goes jogging.
- Right now she's reading a book on anthropology.
- In the last few days she has been studying for a test.
- Recently she's been learning German as a hobby.
- This weekend she'll be working on a paper for her master's degree, playing tennis with a friend, and going to a movie with her boyfriend.

11a Look at the profile outline below. What questions will you need to ask to complete it?

Profile of ________________ (name)

- ________________ is a ________________.
- Before ________________, ________________ had been ________________.
- After finishing work or school, ________________ usually ________________.
- Right now ________________ is reading ________________.
- In the last few days ________________ has been ________________ ________________.
- Recently ________________ has been ________________.
- This weekend ________________ will be ________________.

b **Pair Work** Interview your partner. Choose one or two pieces of information about your partner to tell the class.

LESSON 3

Explain everyday problems

CAN DO

GRAMMAR fronting

Reading

1 **Pair Work** Discuss. What is happening in the photo? Have you ever been in a situation like this? What happened?

2a Read the two letters to an advice column. What advice can you think of?

http://www.advice.com

Problem A

My friend's kids are too spoiled!

My closest friend has two children. The trouble is, they are really spoiled. Every time they come to visit, they jump on the furniture and break things. When I try to say something to my friend, she gives me a dirty look and says, "That's kids for you!" What really irritates me is the fact that my friend just can't see it. I don't know what to do.

Silvia

Problem B

Too much exaggeration?

I recently got a job at a very good company. During the application process, I exaggerated a few details on my resumé. The thing is, I really wanted the job. I knew I could do it and felt that adding a few things to my resumé would give me a better chance. Recently, a colleague of mine who had done the same thing got caught. They fired him. What really worries me is that my company is now promising to check up on all the employees. I am seriously nervous, even though I am doing a good job and my boss likes me. What should I do?

Jake

b Read the advice to Silvia and Jake's problems. Do you agree with the suggestions?

Comments

1 Dear Silvia,

What you need to do is to put yourself in your friend's shoes. She's used to their behavior. You're not. The fact remains that you need to find a solution. One thing you could try is giving the children rewards for good behavior. What might also work is having some games available for them. Maybe there's not enough for the children to do at your house. Good luck!

Faisal

2 Dear Silvia,

There's not much you can do. They're her kids, not yours. But you don't have to put up with that kind of behavior in your house. Why don't you arrange to visit them in her house? That way, if the kids start acting up, you can leave at any time. The point is, she was your friend before the kids, and she can still be your friend now.

Karen

Comments

3 Dear Jake,

I can understand why you fooled the company (you wanted the job). Why you insist on fooling yourself I really don't know. You didn't "exaggerate." You lied. The first thing you must do is go straight to your boss and explain exactly what you did and why you did it. The truth is, if your boss values you and your work, you may get away with it.

Ava

4 Dear Jake,

The fact of the matter is that 19 percent of all job applicants claim skills they don't have, and 28 percent exaggerate the pay from their former jobs. Don't worry about it. Look at it from the company's point of view. Do they really want to go to the trouble of firing you and finding a replacement when they don't really need to? What they really care about is your ability to do the job. Relax, man! You're safe.

Anthony

Grammar | fronting

3 Complete the tasks after the rules in the Active Grammar box.

Active Grammar

1 **Fronting** is rephrasing sentences by moving the object, verb, or adverb to the front of the sentence (before the subject). We sometimes add *what* (or another question word). In Problem A:

The fact that my friend just can't see it really irritates me . . . →

***What really irritates me is** the fact that my friend just can't see it . . .*

Fronting is used:

a. to emphasize the subject (for example, ***the fact** that my friend just can't see it*).

b. sometimes to provide a clear link with the previous sentence: *She told us to go quickly. **This we did.***

Find other examples in Comments 1, 3, and 4.

2. We often use **fronting phrases** (*the trouble is, the question is, the fact of the matter is, the fact remains that*) to emphasize the importance of what we are going to say:

***The trouble is,** they are really spoiled.* (Problem A)

***The thing is,** I really wanted the job.* (Problem B)

Find other examples of **fronting phrases** in Comments 1–4.

American English	British English
spoiled	*spoilt*

See Reference page 129

4 Rewrite the sentences, keeping the meaning the same. Start with the underlined word.

1. Their bad behavior bothers me. What
2. I'm not sure how long he hoped to get away with the lie. How
3. I don't know how she manages with those kids. How
4. She didn't discipline them. That was the problem. The
5. My colleague lost his job. It worries me. What

5 **SPEAKING EXCHANGE** Work in groups of three. Student A: read page 133, Student B: read page 135, and Student C: read page 132. Explain your problems to each other and give advice. Try to use fronting expressions.

What you need to do is encourage your friend to have some fun. Maybe you can . . .

Listening

6a **Pair Work** Tell your partner about problems you have had with everyday machines.

b ▶2.12 Listen. What problems are the people having with their machines?

7 **Pair Work** Imagine there is a problem with an item of technology in your home. Describe it (without mentioning the name of the item), using phrases from the How To box. Your partner guesses what you are talking about and gives advice.

How To:

Describe problems

It keeps (getting jammed).

I can't get it to (make copies).

I don't know how to make it (shut down).

I'm having a problem (turning it on).

This seems to (be stuck).

It won't (turn).

Vocabulary | cause and effect

8 Complete the statements with words and phrases from the box. Then match the problems with each piece of advice.

resulted	source	bring	from	influence	origins	gives	consequence

____ 1. My father was a great ____________ on me, and I've always followed in his footsteps, but now nothing I do is good enough for him. He criticizes me all the time.

____ 2. My obsessive work ethic has ____________ in several problems. I can't sleep or relax, and I get headaches.

____ 3. I dropped out of college. The ____________ of my actions is that my parents won't talk to me now.

____ 4. Most of my problems stem ____________ my laziness. I just can't get motivated to do anything.

a. Overwork ____________ rise to many health problems. You need to get some balance back in your life. Take some time out every day and take up a relaxing hobby.

b. Personal happiness has its ____________ in our achievements. Do something small every day, and you will feel happier and motivated to do more. Take that first step.

c. A child's uncertain future is a major ____________ of stress for parents. They probably can't understand why you have dropped out. Try explaining the whole story from beginning to end.

d. You should try to ____________ about small changes in your relationship with him. Explain that you are an adult now and you need to find your own path in life.

9 **Group Work** Complete the sentences so they are true for you. Compare your answers with other students.

1. ____________ is sometimes a source of stress for me.
2. ____________ influenced me a lot, because ____________.
3. ____________ resulted in my learning English.
4. The consequence of ____________ was ____________.
5. I hope to have an influence on ____________.

Writing

10a Read the essay in the Writing Bank on page 137 and do the exercises.

b Think of a problem or issue, for example—stress, noisy neighbors, unemployment, unhealthy lifestyles, annoying emails, pollution. Make notes about the causes of the problem and the effects it has had on you or others. Try to come up with some solutions.

c Write an essay of 200–250 words about the problem or issue.

Extra Vocabulary Study and Extra Listening Activity in ACTIVEBOOK

Review

1 Find eight mistakes and correct them.

We propose to adopt a new measurement of people's lives. Recently it was explained us that the kingdom of Bhutan measures its citizens' well-being by Gross National Happiness instead of Gross National Product. The country encourages people think about their quality of life, not just money. In many countries, tourism is blamed for destroy the local culture. While the Bhutanese are not accusing anyone of deliberately harm the environment, in Bhutan, tourism is strictly limited.

We suggest to adopt this same idea. We urge people to considering spiritual wealth, as well as money. This approach is guaranteed to opening our eyes to a better way of life.

2 Complete the questions.

1. ________________ (plan) on getting your PhD?
   Yes, I was. It seemed like a good idea, but I didn't have enough money.
2. ________________ (wear) those weird clothes?
   Because I'm supposed to be at a costume party in ten minutes.
3. ________________ (go) when I saw you this afternoon?
   To the bank. But it was closed by the time I got there.
4. ________________ (play) basketball?
   For about ten years. But I only play once a week nowadays.
5. ________________ (live) there long before they kicked him out?
   Yes, he had. Almost 20 years.
6. ________________ (see) what I mean?
   Not exactly. Can you explain it again?

3 Put the words in the box in the correct place in the paragraphs.

would	problem	is
matter	surprises	why

My family is going to visit my mother-in-law next week. The is, we can't stand her cooking! I want to be culturally sensitive—she is from another country—but the fact of the is that the kids and I just can't eat her meals.
Marlene

What me is her cultural insensitivity. The thing, she has to adapt to you, too. Why not take her out to a nice restaurant instead?
Veronica

You're complaining about this I really don't know. All over the world, people are starving. You're lucky enough to have food, so just pretend you like it. If you're desperate, one idea be to train the kids to say "Mmm, delicious."
Ayodele

4 Complete the sentences.

1. Carl Honoré had a great __________ on the Slow Life Movement. Many people followed his ideas.
2. The modern work ethic has __________ in more stressful lifestyles.
3. Twenty-two percent of us suffer from work-related stress. The __________ of this are very serious.
4. Stress at work __________ rise to absenteeism, which is disastrous __________ business.
5. Honoré wants to __________ about a great revolution in lifestyles. His work could have big __________ for humanity.
6. Violence, job insecurity, and overwork are the major __________ of stress in the US.
7. Honoré's philosophy has its __________ in the lifestyles of our ancestors, who didn't work so hard.

Communication | summarize opinions on issues

5a Read the statements. Can any of them be used to describe the photos above?

____ a. Travel is the greatest form of education.
____ b. Marriage is an old-fashioned idea, and it's not necessary these days.
____ c. Money can't make you happy.
____ d. The dominance of any one culture is bad for the world.
____ e. Modern technology has not made the world a better place.
____ f. Rich countries should always give money to poor countries.
____ g. Space exploration is a waste of money.
____ h. As you become older, you become wiser.
____ i. Nature gives us the best things in life.
____ j. Childhood is the happiest time of life.
____ k. For some crimes, the death penalty is appropriate.

b Read the statements again and give each a number from 1 to 5 (1 = disagree completely, 5 = agree completely).

6a **Group Work** Choose five topics from Exercise 5a to discuss. Compare the numbers you gave for each statement and exchange opinions.

I don't think that rich countries should automatically give money to poor countries, but I do think that they should provide aid in some situations . . .

b Report back to the rest of the class: which issues did you talk about? What were the main views and opinions on each?

UNIT 9
People with vision

A

B

C

D

Warm Up

1 **Pair Work** What art forms are represented in the photos? What kinds of art do you prefer and why?

2 Do the words and phrases in bold refer to books, movies, theater, art, or architecture? There may be more than one answer.

1. It was a **spectacular/breathtaking/disappointing** performance.
2. It's **a masterpiece/not one of his best/his finest piece.**
3. The acting was **stereotyped/poor/over the top.**
4. It's a **fantastic/difficult/heavy** read.
5. The style is **contemporary/traditional/art deco.**
6. The special effects were **astonishing/incredible/awful.**
7. He is famous for his **landscapes/portraits/sculptures.**

3 **Group Work** Talk about paintings, movies, books, and other art forms that you like or dislike, using vocabulary from Exercise 2.

My favorite painting is Picasso's Guernica. *I think it's a masterpiece.*

I didn't really enjoy King Kong. *In my opinion, the special effects were pretty disappointing.*

Express a degree of certainty

GRAMMAR collocations with prepositions

CAN DO

Reading

1 **Pair Work** What do you know about the people in the pictures?

Leonardo da Vinci

The Yellow Emperor

Sir Isaac Newton

2 Read the short biographies.

Leonardo da Vinci

As a painter, his legacy of work is indisputably less extensive than other master painters. As an anatomist, he failed to publish his research. As a sculptor, he left us not a single verified sculpture. As a mathematician, he had no significant input into **the development of** the theories of mathematics. As a scientist, his records are disorderly. As a musician, he left little record of his music. As an architect, he left no notable buildings for us to visit. And yet he is popularly held as one of the most important figures of the Italian Renaissance. In the words of Sigmund Freud, "Leonardo da Vinci was like a man who awoke too early in the darkness, while the others were all still asleep."

Most people recognize the *Mona Lisa* or *The Last Supper* as examples of this artist's extraordinary capabilities. However, he was not just an artistic genius. He was also a genius **in the fields of** architecture, engineering, and science. His sketchbooks, with notes often written in mirror form, were full of **ideas for** his inventions. Some were improvements on existing machines; others were new and **ranged from** a primitive tank **to** a human-powered flying machine. These books were to stun the world when they were discovered centuries after his death.

Huang Di

The first sovereign of civilized China, Huang Di, or the Yellow Emperor as he became known, is thought of as the common ancestor of the Chinese people. A semi-legendary figure who is said to have begun his reign around 2697 BC, **in a time of** constant warfare between tribes, Huang Di strove to improve the virtues of people, pacifying by strengthening his army and unifying the tribes. He introduced **the idea of** military discipline, invented the compass to improve his military strategy, and used carts in warfare.

Once he had established peace, he created civilized systems for his people. Among the many inventions **attributed to** him are the calendar, mathematics (he invented numbers and a system for measuring length and weight), music (he invented the flute using bamboo), writing (he invented Chinese characters), boats, carts, and bows and arrows.

His scientific interests also led him to author *The Inner Book of Simple Questions of the Yellow Emperor*, the founding classic of Chinese medicine. His Empress is also **famous for** having been the first to raise silkworms to make clothes with silk.

Sir Isaac Newton

Newton **made** fundamental **contributions to** every area of scientific and mathematical concern in his generation. Born in a rural English village on Christmas Day, 1642, he was so small no one thought he would survive. During his childhood he spent much of his time inventing and building toys. He was distracted at school and did not do particularly well. So his mother, unwilling to pay for his education, brought him home to look after the sheep. However, he was always so busy building gadgets that the sheep would often escape. Eventually, his uncle persuaded his mother to send him to Cambridge University, where he became so **immersed in** his studies that he often forgot to eat or sleep.

When Cambridge was closed for two years due to the plague, Newton went home to **work on** his ideas. He absorbed himself in mathematics and began developing a mathematical theory that would later become calculus. It is a popular belief that **on one occasion** he was sitting under an apple tree when an apple fell on his head, and that this helped him to understand the laws of gravity. It is now thought that perhaps he invented this story later in life in order to exemplify how he **drew** his **inspiration from** everyday events.

3 **Pair Work** Discuss. Which of the people in the reading achieved the most, in your opinion? Which person would you most like to have met? Why?

Grammar | collocations with prepositions

4 Complete the tasks in the Active Grammar box.

Active Grammar

1. Look at the examples of dependent prepositions in bold in the Reading. Write the correct prepositions in the chart.

a. verb + preposition	*range ______ . . . to . . .* *work _____* *attribute _____*
b. verb + object + preposition	*draw inspiration ______* *made contributions _____*
c. noun + preposition	*in the fields _____* *idea _____/_____* *the development _____*
d. adjective + preposition	*(be) famous ______* *(be) immersed _____*
e. prepositional phrases (beginning with a preposition)	*_____ a time of* *_____ one occasion*

2. Write the letter of the correct dependent preposition form next to the phrases below.

_a_ succeed in	__ hope for	__ admiration for
__ improve on	__ specialize in	__ in recognition of
__ of all time	__ a solution to	__ devote your life to
__ in later life	__ the quality of	__ (be) obsessed with
__ make observations about		

See Reference page 130

5 Find expressions in the chart that mean the following:

a. spend your life trying to do something
b. thought to have been achieved or accomplished by someone
c. be worried about something all the time
d. be completely involved in something
e. make something better
f. feeling of great respect or liking for something or someone

6 Circle the correct choices to complete the paragraphs. What is the name of this visionary scientist?

Widely regarded as the greatest scientist of the 20th century, or even (1. *of/all/in*) all time, this man devoted his life (2. *in/on/to*) science. He made major contributions (3. *from/to/for*) the development of quantum mechanics, statistical mechanics, and cosmology. In recognition (4. *for/of/about*) his work, he was awarded the Nobel Prize for Physics in 1921.

In 1905, while working alone in a patent laboratory, he eventually succeeded (5. *to/in/with*) finding a solution (6. *to/at/of*) a problem he had been working (7. *in/for/on*). He developed his own theory of relativity. He later improved (8. *on/to/with*) his own theories until he developed the theory which he became famous (9. *of/about/for*), $E=mc^2$. (10. *In/At/To*) later life, he realized both the positive and negative implications of his work, as nuclear energy and atomic bombs were developed.

7 **Pair Work** Think of other famous "visionaries" or inspirational people. Ask and answer questions about them, using the phrases in the Active Grammar box.

This person was famous for the beautiful music he wrote.

Listening

8 ▶ 2.13 Read the headings on the post-it. Then listen to a radio interview. Make notes under the headings.

1 Discoveries made outside the laboratory

2 The psychology of high achievers

3 Can only creative people be geniuses?

9 **Pair Work** Discuss.

1. Did you find any of the information in the interview surprising?
2. Have you ever come up with the solution to a problem by "sleeping on it"?
3. Do you pursue any creative hobbies or interests?
4. What do you do to take your mind off a problem?

10 Read the words and phrases in the How To box. Then circle the correct choice to complete each statement.

1. It's *debatable/without a doubt* whether Leonardo da Vinci was a genius.
2. It's *not 100 percent certain/undeniably* what or who killed Mozart.
3. The Yellow Emperor was *not clear-cut/unquestionably* a great leader.
4. It's *not clear-cut/irrefutable* why Leonardo wrote in mirror form.
5. Mozart was *not 100 percent certain/irrefutably* exceptionally gifted.
6. The story about Newton's discovery under the apple tree is *questionable/without a doubt*.
7. The novel is *not clear-cut/indisputably* his greatest work.

How To:

Express certainty or uncertainty

certainty	uncertainty
indisputable	*not 100 percent certain*
without a doubt	*questionable*
irrefutable	*debatable*
undeniably	*not clear-cut*
unquestionably	

Speaking

11 **Group Work** Do you agree or disagree with the statements? Explain your views, using phrases from the How To box.

1. Mozart is the most talented musician to have ever lived.
2. Einstein should have kept quiet about his discovery when he realized the implications for nuclear weapons.
3. Being a "genius" generally implies being at least a little crazy. Van Gogh would never have achieved the same recognition if he hadn't suffered a psychological breakdown.
4. Given time and the right encouragement, anyone can become a genius.

LESSON 2

Use colloquial expressions to explain your tastes

CAN DO

GRAMMAR discourse markers

Vocabulary | describing art

1 **Pair Work** Discuss. What sort of art do you like or dislike?

2 Match the sentences on the left with their opposites on the right. Which of the words in bold are used to show personal opinions? Which describe facts?

____ 1. This is an **abstract** painting by Mondrian.
____ 2. This painting is really **striking**. It stands out.
____ 3. I don't like **avant-garde** art. I can't understand it.
____ 4. Don't you find her work really calm and **tranquil**?

a. So you prefer more **traditional** stuff?
b. No way! I think her work is very **disturbing**.
c. Oh, I think that one's **dull**. It doesn't appeal to me.
d. He also did a lot of **figurative** work, didn't he?

3 **Pair Work** Tell your partner about a painting or photograph you like (or don't like). Use phrases from the How To box.

How To:

Say what you like/dislike

Saying what you like	*I've always admired her work.* *I'm really into her work.* *I'm a big fan of his stuff.* *He's one of my all-time favorites.*
Saying what you don't like	*It's not my (kind of) thing.* *It's not my taste.* *It's not my cup of tea.* *I can't relate to it.*

Listening

4a 2.14 Listen to each conversation. Answer the questions.

Conversation 1: Which statement best describes their reaction to the first painting?

a. It's abstract. b. It's disturbing. c. It's striking.

Conversation 2: Which statement best describes their reaction to the second painting?

a. It's disturbing. b. It's fascinating. c. It's dull.

Conversation 3: Which statement is true about their reaction to the third painting?

a. It's their favorite. b. It's disappointing.
c. It's over the top.

b 2.15 Listen. Which painting won the art competition?

a. The portrait of the woman.
b. The portrait of the man.
c. The portrait of the group.

What does the man think about the winning portrait? ____________________

Grammar | discourse markers

5 Read the Active Grammar box and complete the chart.

Active Grammar

1. Discourse markers are words and expressions that help us organize what we are saying or writing. They also show our attitude toward the subject.

   Look at the following phrases from the Listening and put the words **in bold** in the correct place in the chart.

   *. . . **as I was saying,** it really does look like a photo . . .*
   *. . . the expression on her face **is kind of** intense . . .*
   *. . . **it sort of** looks like a photo . . .*
   *. . . **to be honest,** it's not really my taste . . .*
   *. . . **to tell you the truth,** I still wouldn't want it hanging on my bedroom wall.*

Focusing on the main topic	Returning to the main point (what was said before didn't matter)	Returning to a previous line of discussion
Introducing a strong opinion or criticism	**Softening an opinion or criticism**	**Making additional (often contrasting) points**

2. Look at the phrases below and add them to the chart.

more or less	mind you	in fact	frankly,	as a matter of fact
at any rate	regarding	as for	anyway	as far as ___ is concerned,
anyway, what I was going to say was				

See Reference page 130

6 Circle the best choice to complete each sentence.

1. A: *To be honest/As far as it's concerned/Regarding*, I don't like Impressionism very much.
   B: Neither do I. *As for it/What I was going to say/At any rate*, I think it's been over done.
2. A: Pollock's technique of dripping paint onto canvas was *as for/anyway/kind of* strange.
   B: I agree. *More or less,/ Mind you,/As regards* his work did revolutionize modern art.
3. A: I love performance art. *Sort of/Regarding/As a matter of fact*, David Blaine's my hero.
   B: David Blaine? The magician? *Anyway, what I was going to say was/Frankly,/As I was saying*, I think he's crazy!
4. A: I love Spanish art. *Kind of/In fact/As for* Picasso, I think he was the greatest of all time.
   B: Well, yes, he *more or less/as regards/to tell you the truth* invented modern art.
5. A: *As far as it's concerned/Regarding/Anyway,* photography, Cindy Sherman is currently the most famous artist.
   B: Really? *In fact/As I was saying/To tell you the truth*, I've never heard of her.

Speaking

7 **Pair Work** Discuss.

1. Do you ever go to art exhibitions? If so, what was the last one you went to? Did you like it?
2. Do you have a favorite artist? Why do you like his or her work?

Reading

8a Look at the picture. What is happening?

b Read the article and answer the questions that follow.

Now you see it . . .

No wonder the man in Munch's *The Scream* is screaming. He keeps getting stolen. The famous painting was stolen in 1994 and again ten years later, both times from museums in Norway. Apparently, security was extremely poor. Officials thought the painting was so famous that it wouldn't be stolen. Wrong.

The world of art theft is not, as you might imagine, populated with stylish **aesthetes**, **masterminding** their operations from tax-free **hideouts**. Art thieves are **thugs**, according to a new book by Charley Hill. Hill was an undercover policeman whose job was to **track down** stolen paintings. He says that the people who steal paintings were usually stealing wheels from cars a few years earlier. He describes priceless Vermeers being **stuffed** into the back of cars, Gainsboroughs being passed around by drug dealers with dirty hands, and a particularly bad end to one of Henry Moore's huge sculptures. The bronze, *King and Queen*, a masterpiece by Moore, was too heavy for the thieves to move, so they took out a chainsaw and cut off the heads, thinking they might be worth something.

Hill's is an adventure story fit for any James Bond fan. In 1986 he **cracked a case** in which 11 valuable paintings had been stolen from Russborough House near Dublin. In order to rescue *The Scream*, Hill posed as a buyer for the J. Paul Getty Museum in LA: bow tie, big suit, even bigger Mercedes. He also had to learn everything about the painting, or should we say paintings: there are four versions of *The Scream*. He even memorized the patterns of wax droplets left on one version of the painting when Munch blew out a candle one night.

The artworks usually turn up, sometimes many years later, though the police don't always catch the thief. Even rarer is when a gentleman thief—one who steals art for personal pleasure only—is caught. In 2003, a waiter, Stephane Breitwieser from Switzerland, was found guilty of stealing 69 artworks from museums since 1995. He told the court he did it for the love of art. His **haul** was worth over $1 billion—not bad for a waiter.

1. Why was *The Scream* so badly protected?
2. What are Vermeers and Gainsboroughs, and what happened to them?
3. What did Hill have to do to find *The Scream*?
4. Who is Stephane Breitwieser, and why is he unusual among art thieves?

9 **Pair Work** Discuss.

1. Would you like Charley Hill's job? Why or why not?
2. Do you think Hill's book sounds interesting?
3. What type of person do you think Stephane Breitwieser might be?
4. What type of people collect art? Do you think it would be an enjoyable hobby?

10a Answer the questions.

1. What does *thug* (line 10) mean?
2. How does the article describe the people who steal paintings? How does this help us guess the meaning of *thug*?

b Answer the same questions for the following words and phrases: *masterminding* (line 8), *aesthetes* (line 8), *hideout* (line 9), *track down* (line 11), *stuffed* (line 15), *crack a case* (line 23), *haul* (line 39).

Respond to hypothetical questions

CAN DO

GRAMMAR unreal past

Writing

1a Choose one of the photos. How does it make you feel? What does it remind you of? What do you think is happening? Imagine that you are in the scene. Write a paragraph about what you are feeling and doing.

b Read your paragraph to the rest of the class. Were your impressions similar or different?

Speaking

2 **Pair Work** Discuss.

1. Do you have a camera or a camera phone? How often do you use it?
2. What do you think makes a good photo? Can you think of any tips for taking better photos?

Reading

3a **SPEAKING EXCHANGE** Student A: read the article on page 132. Student B: read the article on page 134. As you read, note what the article says about:

1. the best time to do it
2. stories
3. the local culture
4. learning from professionals

b Tell your partner about the main ideas in your article and your answers to Exercise 3a.

4 **Pair Work** Discuss.

1. What do you think of the advice in your article? Was it interesting, obvious, or surprising?
2. Which sounds easier—being a photographer or being a travel writer?
3. Would you like to be a travel writer or a photographer? Why or why not?

Grammar | unreal past

5 Complete the tasks after each expression in the Active Grammar box.

Active Grammar

Wish* or *If only

*If only **I'd gone** on that trip.*

1. Find more examples of these expressions in the introductions to your articles in Exercise 3a.
2. What verb tense follows *wish* or *if only* to talk about (a) the present? (b) the past?

It's high time* or *It's about time

*It's high time we **visited** Tokyo.*

3. Find examples of these expressions in the introduction on page 138 and section 1 on page 140.
4. Does *It's high time* or *It's about time* mean (a) something should be happening now, but it isn't OR (b) something is happening on time?
5. What verb tense follows *It's high time* or *It's about time*?

Would rather

*I would rather **go**.*
*I would rather they **left**.*

6. Find examples of *would rather* in section 5 on page 138 and section 2 on page 140.
7. What verb form follows *would rather* if the person speaking and the subject are (a) the same? (b) different?

What if* or *Suppose

*Suppose you **had taken** that job as a photographer. Would you be happier now?*

8. Find more examples of these expressions in section 1 on page 138 and section 3 on page 140.
9. What verb tense follows *what if* or *suppose* to talk about an imaginary situation in the (a) present? (b) past? (c) future?

See Reference page 130

6 Complete the second sentence so that it has a similar meaning to the first. Use the corrrect form of the verb in parentheses.

1. We should start our journals. (begin)
   It's high __________ writing our journals.
2. What if you had the chance to become a travel journalist? (offer)
   Suppose someone __________ a job as a travel journalist?
3. Please stop taking photos! (take)
   We'd rather __________ photos.
4. I should have sent in my story for the writing competition. (enter)
   If only __________ the competition, I might have won!
5. I'd love to be able to take good photos. (be)
   I wish __________ a good photographer.
6. We should select the photos for my new travel book together. (choose)
   I'd rather __________ photos together.
7. You should finish writing that article soon. (finish)
   It's about __________ that article.

7 **Pair Work** Complete the sentences so they are true for you. Then share them with your partner. Ask your partner questions about his or her sentences.

It's high time I ___. It's about time ___. I wish ___.
I'd rather ___ than ___. Suppose ___. If only ___.

It's high time I applied to graduate school.

What are you going to study?

Speaking

8a **Pair Work** Think about the situations below and discuss them. Try to use some of the expressions in the How To box. Extend the discussion for as long as possible.

Ex: A: *What if you were alone in the house and it suddenly caught fire?*
B: *I'd probably try to save my photos.*
A: *Why? Wouldn't you rather save something valuable?*
B: *No way! I'd rather save the photos because they represent a lot of happy memories.*

How To:

Respond to hypothetical questions

positively	***It's highly likely*** *I'd agree.* *I* ***would probably*** *agree to that.* *I* ***would consider*** *doing that.* *I* ***suppose*** *I* ***might*** *do that.*
negatively	*I* ***probably wouldn't*** *accept.* ***It's unlikely*** *I'd be able to do that.* ***There's no way*** *I'd do that.*

1. Suppose you could write great novels or paint great pictures or sing beautifully. Which would you choose?
2. What if you could travel to any one period in the past? Which would you choose?
3. What if you could be Leonardo da Vinci, Albert Einstein, or Mozart for one day? Who would you be?
4. Suppose a film director asked to make a film about your life? Would you accept? Who would you like to play you?
5. Suppose you could interview one famous person for a magazine. Who would it be?
6. What if someone asked you to participate in a reality TV show?

b Think of two more hypothetical questions to ask your partner. Start your questions with *What if . . .* or *Suppose . . . ?*

Writing

9 Choose one of the situations in Exercise 8a. Imagine that it really happened. Write the story in about 150 words.

Extra Vocabulary Study and Extra Listening Activity in ACTIVEBOOK

Review

1 Choose the correct phrase to complete each sentence.

____ 1. Doris Lessing won the Nobel Prize for literature in recognition
____ 2. Stephen Pinker, a well-known academic, is a master in the fields
____ 3. Many people have drawn inspiration from
____ 4. Kurosawa was one of the greatest film directors of
____ 5. Da Vinci's abilities ranged from
____ 6. Thomas Edison succeeded in
____ 7. US pilot Amelia Earhart devoted her life to

a. of her contribution to the novel.
b. the life of Helen Keller.
c. all time.
d. flying.
e. painting to designing weapons.
f. registering 1,093 patents for new inventions.
g. of both cognitive science and linguistics.

2 Complete the conversation with the words and expressions in the box.

more or less	regarding	be honest	in fact	as far as my work is concerned	kind

A: Rachel, how are you feeling now that you've won the Turner Prize?
B: Thrilled. To ____________ (1.), I never expected to win. I ____________ (2.) of knew I had a chance, but it was still a big surprise.
A: How will this affect you?
B: ____________ (3.), it won't affect me at all. I already have three exhibitions planned. ____________ (4.) the money, it'll mean I can focus on my work.
A: We hear you'll be making videos, rather than painting. Is this true?
B: That's ____________ (5.) true. I'll be making videos, but I'll still paint. ____________ (6.), my next exhibition will be mainly paintings.
A: Thank you, Rachel. We're looking forward to it.

3 Circle the correct word or phrase.

1. What if we *are leaving/left/would have left* really early? Would we arrive on time?
2. I would rather *know/to know/knowing* the truth now than later.
3. I wish I *will/can/could* dance better.
4. It's high time we *had gone/went/go*.
5. She wishes she *had gotten up/got up/was getting up* earlier yesterday.
6. Suppose you *are running/run/have run* into trouble, what will you do?
7. It's about time they *learn/learned/had learned* to act like adults.
8. We wish you *didn't bring/hadn't brought/wouldn't bring* your dog yesterday.

4 Complete the sentences with suitable words and phrases with meanings similar to those in parentheses. Use the letters shown.

1. It was a disaster—a really d__________ performance! (*poor*)
2. The show is quite funny. The characters are really o__________ t__________ t__________. (*exaggerated*)
3. He does have interesting ideas, but his style makes it a pretty h__________ read. (*hard work*)
4. The decor hasn't changed since the 1980s, so it's not very c__________. (*modern* or *up-to-date*)
5. Michelangelo's *David* is without a doubt his f__________ p__________. (*best work*)
6. The i__________ special effects were what made the film such a success. (*unbelievable*)

Communication | collaborate on a proposal

Clarence Birdseye

Chester Carlson

5a ▶2.16 Listen and mark the statements true (*T*) or false (*F*).

____ 1. Clarence Birdseye was the first person to put food in salt water to freeze it.
____ 2. The equipment for his experiments was cheap.
____ 3. Birdseye sold the first modern freezer for $22 million.
____ 4. Chester Carlson's job was to invent a machine to make copies.
____ 5. Carlson found his work difficult because of his own health problems.
____ 6. The first commercial photocopier was made over 20 years after Carlson had first invented the machine.

b Listen again to check your answers.

6 **Pair Work** Discuss.

1. Would you describe frozen food as an "original" idea?
2. Can you think of any other popular products that are based on earlier inventions?

7a **Pair Work** You are planning a new business venture and need to persuade the rest of the class to invest in your idea. Choose one of the ideas on the right (or come up with an idea of your own) and plan how you are going to "sell" it to the rest of the class.

b Write the name of the product, service, or movie, and a short summary of the main ideas behind it, its main benefits, and other important features. Then present your proposal to the rest of the class. Ask and answer questions about each proposal.

A NEW PRODUCT
You have invented a jacket that can change color and ____________. Made of the latest high-tech material, and with a range of ten colors, the jacket takes five seconds to change color. It also has special ____________. . . .

A NEW SERVICE
Doitforyou.com offers to help you with ____________. Users pay a fixed monthly fee and can use the service as often as they wish. Additional benefits include ____________. . . .

A NEW MOVIE
It is 2100. The world has become ____________. Only one person can save the planet because he or she has the key to the secret ____________. The problem is that there is a terrible ____________ who doesn't want the world to be saved. . . .

UNIT 10
Expressing feelings

A

B

C

D

Warm Up

1 **Pair Work** Discuss. How do you think the people in the photos are feeling? Why?

2 Check that you understand the meaning of the idioms in bold. Which idioms apply to the people in the photos? Then match the sentences on the left with the sentences on the right.

____ 1. She was **at her wits end** with worry.
____ 2. He failed his exam, so he's a bit **down in the dumps**.
____ 3. They saw the same car at a much lower price, so now they're **kicking themselves**.
____ 4. He is very **pleased with himself** for winning the game.
____ 5. I'm **of two minds** about whether to accept the invitation.
____ 6. Try not to get so **wound up**—it's only a traffic jam.

a. He deserves **a pat on the back**.
b. Just **chill out**!
c. We should try to **cheer him up**.
d. But they can't **do anything about it** now.
e. We went out to **take her mind off** the problem.
f. I just can't **make my mind up**.

LESSON 1 Discuss how feelings affect you

CAN DO

GRAMMAR modals (and verbs with similar meanings)

Listening

1 **Pair Work** Discuss.

1. Do you think your outlook can affect what happens to you in life? How?
2. Do you consider yourself optimistic? Explain.

2 ▶ 2.17 Listen to the interview and choose the correct phrase to complete each sentence.

1. Optimists and pessimists are predisposed to ____.
   a. view events similarly b. view events differently
2. Optimists believe that ____.
   a. they are responsible for the good things that happen
   b. good things happen by chance
3. Pessimists ____.
   a. are more depressed than optimists
   b. are more likely to be depressed than optimists
4. Positive patterns of thinking ____.
   a. are inherited b. can be learned
5. Cognitive restructuring is a way to change ____.
   a. patterns of thought b. a pessimist into an optimist

3 **Pair Work** Discuss.

1. Do you agree with what Dr. Bright says about optimists and pessimists?
2. Do you think that cognitive restructuring makes sense for someone who has a pessimistic outlook?
3. Do you think it's possible for someone to be both an optimist and a pessimist?
4. After listening to the interview, do you consider yourself an optimist or a pessimist? Why?

Grammar | modals (and verbs with similar meanings)

4 Look at the way the words in bold are used in the sentences below. Match them to their correct usage in the Active Grammar box on page 117.

____ 1. He **can't** see the positive in anything.
____ 2. He still **won't** let me forget that incident.
____ 3. There **must** have been some other reason for the accident.
____ 4. It was proof that more good things **will** happen to you.
____ 5. A person with a negative outlook is more **likely** to be depressed.
____ 6. See it as proof that more good things **are bound to** happen to you.
____ 7. You **might** think about whether they are due to something you did.
____ 8. You **must** guard against assuming that you are responsible.
____ 9. I **shouldn't** be too bummed about that?
____ 10. Think of extenuating circumstances that **might** have contributed to the game.
____ 11. And **can** I ask you about your name?
____ 12. We're **supposed to** think positive thoughts.

Active Grammar

1. ***will***
   a. for predictions:
   Do you think the president will win re-election?
   b. for willingness or unwillingness:
   I'll get that for you.
   He won't pay the bills.
2. ***might***
   c. to talk about possibility:
   Sonya might phone later.
   d. to make suggestions (polite):
   You might try asking your brother.
3. ***must, can't***
   e. for obligation:
   You must be at the office by 8 A.M.
   You can't leave before 5 P.M.
   f. for deduction:
   There must be some kind of problem.
   That can't be the manager—he's far too young.
4. ***can***
   g. for permission:
   Can we leave our bags here?
   h. for possibility or impossibility:
   We can't all fit in one car.
5. ***(be) supposed to***
   i. to talk about what you have to do according to rules or regulations:
   We are supposed to be at the presentation.
6. ***(be) bound to***
   j. for future prediction of certainty:
   She's bound to give the secret away.
7. ***(be) likely to***
   k. for probability:
   You're not likely to pass.
8. ***ought to, need to, should***
   l. for obligation, duty, or necessity:
   Do you think we ought to tell them?
   Do we need to make a reservation?
   You really should contact the office.

See Reference page 131

5 **Pair Work** Tell your partner about: 1) three things you should do this week; 2) what you think your best friend is likely to be doing right now; 3) how you think teachers can best motivate their students; and 4) how you think people's lives will change in the future.

Vocabulary | outlook and attitude

6a Check you understand the phrases in bold and complete the questionnaire.

HOW OPTIMISTIC ARE YOU?

How strongly do you agree or disagree with the statements? Use the scale below.

1 strongly disagree
2 disagree
3 neither agree nor disagree
4 agree
5 strongly agree

____ 1. When something I have tried doesn't work, I try to think of new ways to solve the problem.
____ 2. I rarely feel lonely, even when I am by myself.
____ 3. When I'm **going through** a tough time, I turn to my friends and family.
____ 4. I try to **look on the bright side**, even when things are not going my way.
____ 5. When I meet someone new, I assume that he or she will like me.
____ 6. I try to learn from my failures, but I don't **dwell** on them.
____ 7. There are a lot of things that can go wrong, but **chances are** that they won't.
____ 8. I am fairly good at relaxing after I leave work.
____ 9. I **tend to trust** people until they give me a reason not to.
____ 10. You shouldn't take life's problems seriously. Usually things will **work out in the long run**.
____ 11. It's good to look at life with a sense of humor.
____ 12. I see problems as challenges.

b **SPEAKING EXCHANGE** Read the results of the questionnaire on page 133. Compare your answers with other students. Do you agree with the results?

Reading

7 **Pair Work** Discuss whether you agree or disagree with the following statement: You can achieve your dream if you try hard enough, no matter what your limitations are.

8 Read the article.

Flo Fox

I try to set an example by taking the negative and making it positive—both in life and in my work. —Flo Fox

Blind photographer might seem like an oxymoron. How could a person who cannot see possibly take pictures? Flo Fox is among the extraordinary people in this unique profession.

Flo Fox was born blind in one eye. She has joked that this automatically made her a photographer, since she never had to close one eye to take a picture! She bought her first 35 mm camera in 1972 and carried it everywhere she went in New York City. She became a street photographer, particularly drawn to ironic images and subjects that have historical value.

In 1975, Flo Fox lost vision in her good eye and was declared legally blind. Nonetheless, she continued to take pictures. If that weren't a challenge enough, it was right around this time that she was diagnosed with multiple sclerosis and started losing control of her limbs. She was determined not to let her physical limitations affect her career. Instead of walking the streets of New York City with a cane, she drove around in a motorized scooter and continued to seek out subjects for her art. Despite her disabilities, she also managed to travel extensively and document her experiences through her photography.

Flo Fox has taken over 100,000 photographs in her career. Her work has been published in various books and magazines. She has participated in numerous exhibits. Her work is in the permanent collections of the Brooklyn Museum and the Smithsonian Museum. She has given seminars on her photography. She has even hosted a photography show on cable television.

Today Flo Fox is confined to a wheelchair, most of her body immobilized. But she still takes a camera with her wherever she goes. Although she can't take pictures herself, she instructs her attendants and friends on what subjects to shoot and exactly how to do it.

Jimmy Dean once said, "I can't change the direction of the wind, but I can adjust my sails to always reach my destination." Flo Fox has consistently and inspirationally adjusted her sails to realize her dreams. She indeed has an outstanding talent for making negatives into positives!

9 **Pair Work** Discuss the meaning of the following statements.

1. Flo Fox has consistently and inspirationally adjusted her sails to realize her dreams.
2. She indeed has an outstanding talent for making negatives into positives.

Speaking

10a **Group Work** Think about a dream you would like to realize or a goal you would like to achieve. Make a few notes about the following:

1. What is your dream?
2. Why is it important?
3. How will you go about achieving it?
4. Who will help you?
5. What have you done in the past that could help you?
6. How will you motivate yourself?

b Tell each other about your dream or goal. Try to offer advice on how your classmates might achieve their goals.

Make guesses about imaginary situations

GRAMMAR modals of deduction (past and present)

Listening

1 **Pair Work** What is happening in the photos? What would it be like to be there? What problems might there be?

2 2.18 Listen to the conversations. Then listen again and answer the questions.

1. What difficulties with early flights does the speaker mention?
2. What doubts does he think the pilot had?
3. When Machu Picchu was discovered by modern explorers, how was the actual site different from now?
4. What positive and negative emotions does the speaker think Gagarin had?

Grammar | modals of deduction (past and present)

3 Look at the modals of deduction below and read the Audioscript on page 143. Can you find any examples of the modals?

must be, must have been *couldn't be, couldn't have been*
might feel, might have felt *could happen, could have happened*
can't have, can't have been *may live, may have lived*

4 Answer the questions and read the rule in the Active Grammar box.

Active Grammar

1. Which three modals from Exercise 3 have similar meanings?
2. Which modals mean that something is not possible?
3. Which modal means we are sure about something (in the positive)?
4. How are the meanings of *must be* and *must have been* different?

We can also use *will be* to make a guess about the present when we are almost sure that something is true because of habit or deduction.

That'll be John on the phone. He always calls at 6:30.

See Reference page 131

5 What is the difference in meaning (if any) between the two options *in italics* in the sentences below?

1. He *can't/shouldn't* be happy about his exam result. He *normally does/could've done* better.
2. You *couldn't/can't* have stayed awake all night. You never do that.
3. He *might be/could have been* hungry—that would explain the crying.
4. They *may/might* have found the gold.

Speaking

6a **SPEAKING EXCHANGE** Look at the photos on page 135. Discuss what you think is happening or has happened and why.

b Read the story behind each photo on page 133. Were your speculations correct?

Reading

7 **Group Work** Read the introduction on the right. What do you think "some of the biggest highs" and "some of the worst lows" might be?

8 **Pair Work** Read the book review and discuss whether you think the statements that follow are true or false. Give reasons.

***Esquire* magazine interviewed 61 people who had experienced some of the biggest highs and the worst lows known to humanity. The result is a book called *Esquire Presents: What It Feels Like*.**

So what does it feel like . . . ?

1 As we watch James Bond jump out of a plane, shoot 28 bad guys in 5 seconds flat, mix a perfect cocktail and get the girl, most of us know that real life just isn't like this. We're never going to win the Nobel Prize, walk on the Moon, win the lottery, or get attacked by grizzly bears. And that's why *Esquire* magazine decided to find out what these things really feel like.

2 Thanks to Buzz Aldrin, we can share the thrill of walking on the Moon. He describes, "powdery dust . . . the sky velvety black . . . surreal," and his feelings of responsibility: "If we made a mistake, we would regret it for quite a while." Aldrin's account gives us just the right blend of emotion and cold, hard fact. Aldrin's story is, of course, extremely well-known. One of the strengths of *Esquire Presents: What It Feels Like* is that it also covers normal, unexceptional people who find themselves in exceptional circumstances.

3 Max Dearing tells us what it feels like to be struck by lightning: "I was absolutely frozen, just as cold as I've ever been in my entire life, but then part of me was incredibly hot, too. I saw these red flashing lights, and I kept thinking, "It's a fire truck! A fire truck!" as if I were a little kid. Then there was the most incredible noise I'd ever heard."

4 If Dearing's experience is shocking (literally and metaphorically) because of its sudden life-changing violence, Craig Strobeck's story is altogether more terrifying because it affects every minute of his life. Strobeck describes what it feels like to have an obsessive-compulsive disorder. He has to take two-and-a-half-hour showers. He runs out of hot water but doesn't stop. He cleans every inch of his body a thousand times, and sometimes he gets back in the shower because one area just doesn't feel clean enough.

5 Possibly the strangest experience described in the book, though, is that of Geoffrey Petkovich. He went over Niagara Falls, one of the world's largest waterfalls, in a barrel. He did it "for a bit of fun," though it was a pretty bumpy ride. With him in the barrel were two cans of beer, a packet of cigarettes, and two hours' worth of oxygen in tanks, just in case the barrel sank.

6 Petkovich's story is an example of the book's humorous tone, but its editor, A. J. Jacobs, thinks *Esquire Presents: What It Feels Like* has a serious message. "The guy who was buried under 50 feet of snow in an avalanche says that nowadays he can hit his thumb with a hammer and it doesn't bother him. He's just happy to be here." The same is true for most of the people in this fascinating book.

1. The book was published so that ordinary people could read about extraordinary experiences.
2. The book is mainly about famous people's achievements.
3. Buzz Aldrin talks about his regrets.
4. Geoffrey Petkovich is probably a fun-loving person.
5. The book is a serious, academic text.

Vocabulary | strong feelings

9 Put the adjectives in bold in the correct box in the chart. Use a dictionary if necessary.

1. You've just been offered the best job in the world. You must be absolutely **thrilled**!
2. One thing that makes me **furious** is when people litter.
3. I was **taken aback** when they asked me to be the team captain. I hadn't expected it at all.
4. She was **ecstatic** when she finally passed her driving test.
5. I feel completely **indifferent** about that issue; I don't care one way or the other.
6. They split up after ten years together, and now they're both **miserable**.
7. I know math isn't your favorite subject, but do you have to look so **uninterested**?
8. She was **terrified** when she saw the spider in her bed!
9. I was **flabbergasted** when they told me I'd won the lottery.
10. When she won the award, she was **dumbstruck**. She just couldn't believe it!
11. He was **outraged** by your terrible behavior.
12. We're **delighted** that you can come.
13. When the plumber didn't show up again I was **livid**. I'd taken the day off work.
14. Walking down the dark deserted streets, they were **petrified**.
15. We were a little **upset** that you didn't call to say you'd be late.

1. happy	2. unhappy	3. neither happy nor unhappy
4. scared	**5. surprised**	**6. angry**

10 **Pair Work** How would you feel in these situations? Why? Try to use adjectives you haven't used before.

1. You won the Nobel Prize for Physics.
2. You were chosen to go to the International Space Station.
3. You were caught in the middle of a lightning storm.
4. You were offered a job as a model for a clothing company in Milan.
5. You found a large box full of gold coins under your floor.
6. Your neighbor played loud music every night and would not turn it down when asked to.
7. You saw a tiger wandering around your local supermarket.

Describe a childhood memory

CAN DO

GRAMMAR uses of *would*

Listening

1 **Pair Work** Discuss. Which of the topics in the box do you remember from your childhood? How did they make you feel?

playing sports	moving
playing games	babysitting
making friends	taking tests
changing schools	
summer vacation	
spending time alone	
staying with grandparents	
birth of a brother or sister	
arguing with friends or family	

2 ▶2.19 Listen. Which of the topics does each speaker mention? Do any of the stories remind you of experiences from your own childhood?

3 Listen again and answer the questions.

1. Did Speaker 1 find it easy to get along with other children? Why or why not?
2. How has her experience shaped her character?
3. What was bad about Speaker 2's experience?
4. What smells, sensations, and colors does Speaker 3 mention?
5. What was different about the breakfasts she had on vacation?
6. How did playing in the woods make Speaker 4 feel?

Reading

4a Look at the picture. Where do you think the story is set? What do you think it is about? How do you think the girl is feeling?

b Read the excerpt from *The House on Mango Street*. Were your ideas correct?

5 **Pair Work** How did the story make you feel? What do you think life is going to be like in the house on Mango Street?

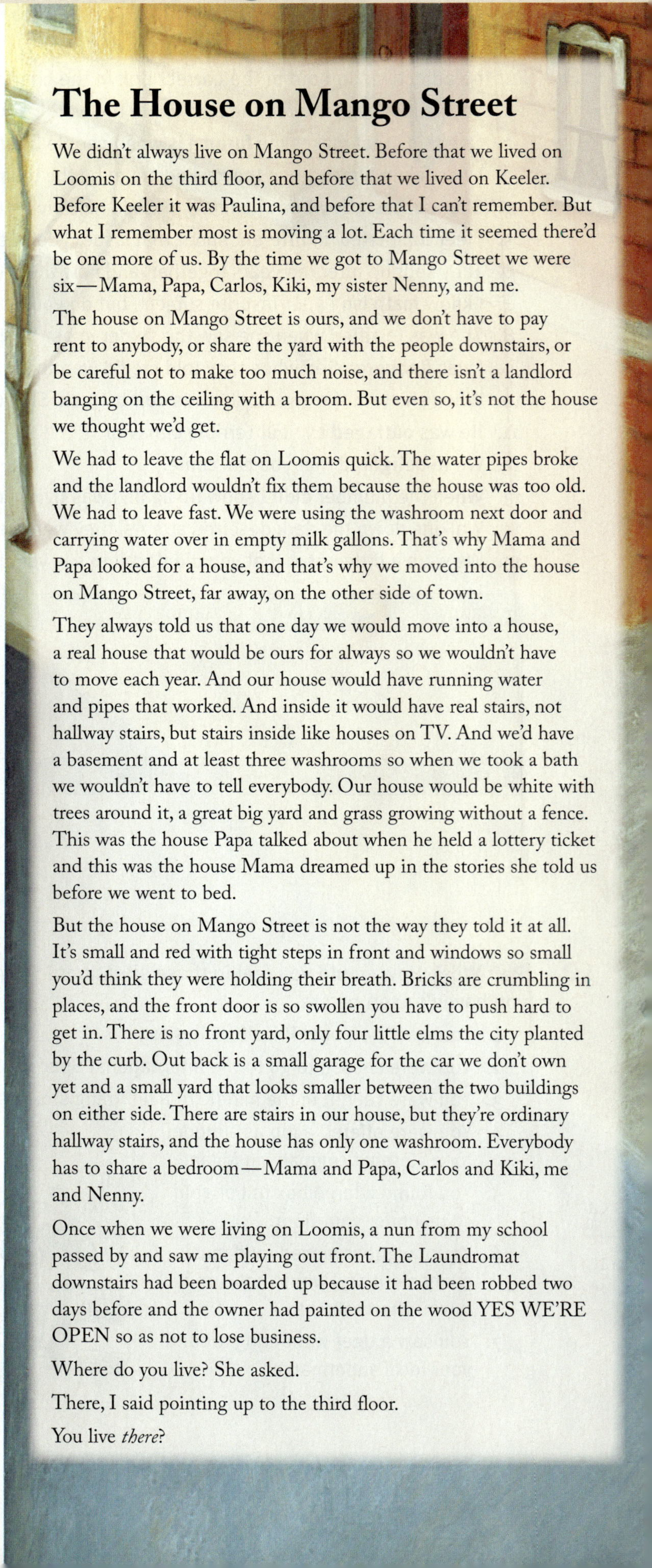

The House on Mango Street

We didn't always live on Mango Street. Before that we lived on Loomis on the third floor, and before that we lived on Keeler. Before Keeler it was Paulina, and before that I can't remember. But what I remember most is moving a lot. Each time it seemed there'd be one more of us. By the time we got to Mango Street we were six—Mama, Papa, Carlos, Kiki, my sister Nenny, and me.

The house on Mango Street is ours, and we don't have to pay rent to anybody, or share the yard with the people downstairs, or be careful not to make too much noise, and there isn't a landlord banging on the ceiling with a broom. But even so, it's not the house we thought we'd get.

We had to leave the flat on Loomis quick. The water pipes broke and the landlord wouldn't fix them because the house was too old. We had to leave fast. We were using the washroom next door and carrying water over in empty milk gallons. That's why Mama and Papa looked for a house, and that's why we moved into the house on Mango Street, far away, on the other side of town.

They always told us that one day we would move into a house, a real house that would be ours for always so we wouldn't have to move each year. And our house would have running water and pipes that worked. And inside it would have real stairs, not hallway stairs, but stairs inside like houses on TV. And we'd have a basement and at least three washrooms so when we took a bath we wouldn't have to tell everybody. Our house would be white with trees around it, a great big yard and grass growing without a fence. This was the house Papa talked about when he held a lottery ticket and this was the house Mama dreamed up in the stories she told us before we went to bed.

But the house on Mango Street is not the way they told it at all. It's small and red with tight steps in front and windows so small you'd think they were holding their breath. Bricks are crumbling in places, and the front door is so swollen you have to push hard to get in. There is no front yard, only four little elms the city planted by the curb. Out back is a small garage for the car we don't own yet and a small yard that looks smaller between the two buildings on either side. There are stairs in our house, but they're ordinary hallway stairs, and the house has only one washroom. Everybody has to share a bedroom—Mama and Papa, Carlos and Kiki, me and Nenny.

Once when we were living on Loomis, a nun from my school passed by and saw me playing out front. The Laundromat downstairs had been boarded up because it had been robbed two days before and the owner had painted on the wood YES WE'RE OPEN so as not to lose business.

Where do you live? She asked.

There, I said pointing up to the third floor.

You live *there*?

> *There.* I had to look to where she pointed—the third floor, the paint peeling, wooden bars Papa had nailed on the windows so we wouldn't fall out. You live *there*? The way she said it made me feel like nothing. *There.* I lived *there.* I nodded.
>
> I knew then I had to have a house. A real house. One I could point to. But this isn't it. The house on Mango Street isn't it. For the time being, Mama says. Temporary, says Papa. But I know how those things go.
>
> Sandra Cisneros

Grammar | uses of *would*

6 Match the example sentences in the Active Grammar box to the different uses of *would.*

Active Grammar

____ 1. *Each time there'**d** be one more of us.*

____ 2. *The landlord **wouldn't** fix them.*

____ 3. *They always told us that one day we **would** move into a real house.*

____ 4. *We packed all the books in wooden boxes so that they **wouldn't** get damaged.*

____ 5. *We'**d** have moved to a different area if we'd been able to afford it.*

____ 6. ***Would** you shut the window, please?*

____ 7. *I wish they **wouldn't** make so much noise at night.*

a. polite request
b. recurring situation in the past
c. past purpose or reason (often used after *so that*)
d. imagined situation
e. strong wish that someone would or wouldn't do something
f. past intention or expectation (reported)
g. refusal

American English	British English
move	*move house*

See Reference page 131

7 Add *would* or *wouldn't* to the following sentences (as appropriate).

1. If you like to follow me, I'll show you to your rooms.
2. I have more time for work if you took care of the kids more often.
3. When we were alone at home, we always cook for ourselves.
4. He never help me with my homework.
5. If only he answer the phone, I could explain what happened.
6. We hid the package in the cabinet so that she notice it.

8 **Pair Work** Complete the sentences and compare your ideas with other students.

Ex: When I was ten years old, I thought *I would grow up to be a doctor* .

When we were young, my friends and I would ____________.
I wish people wouldn't always ____________.
When I was a child my parents wouldn't ____________.
Would you mind if I ____________?
If I were younger (or older), I'd ____________.

Reading

9 Read the stories from a website and write a title for each one.

Stories from Childhood

We asked you to send in stories about some of your earliest childhood memories:

____

I have a vivid recollection of walking to school when I was about ten years old. Every morning I would meet my childhood sweetheart at the corner of the street and carry her backpack all the way to the girls' school gate. In the afternoon, I would wait for her outside the same gate. We would walk home together singing "You Were Made for Me" by Freddie and the Dreamers.

____

I'll always remember my grandfather bringing a newly born black sheep up to the house one time. He let me hold him without completely letting go because the little ball of curls was wriggling like an eel. I was five years old and had never seen a black sheep. His skull was hard as a rock. Later my grandfather told me I was like that little black sheep . . . hard-headed and very special.

____

My earliest memory is of my dad carrying me on his shoulders. On Sundays, we would often go for an afternoon walk, and when I got tired he would carry me. I felt I could see the entire world. And I could . . . my three-year-old world, at least.

____

One memory that sticks in my mind is of my brother and me when we were younger. We generally spent most of our time fighting. We were always chasing each other around the house hitting each other and throwing things. But one night we were staying at my aunt's house, and I was sad about something. I just remember crying into my brother's arms as we were going to bed. I can't even remember now what I was so sad about, but the important thing is that I remember knowing he was there for me, and being comforted by him. Looking back, it's hard to believe what happened that night.

____

One of my earliest memories was of being scared to death because I thought that I'd been abandoned in the hospital ward. I had my tonsils removed when I was two and a half and had to stay overnight by myself. My parents kept telling me that they'd come to take me home "in the morning when the sun shines." The problem was that the next morning, it was raining!

10 Cover the Reading. Think of different ways to complete the phrases in the How To box. Then compare your ideas with the Reading.

How To:

Describe a childhood memory

Introducing the story	• *I have a ___ recollection of . . .* • *I'll ___ remember . . .* • *One of my ___ memories is of . . .*
Background	• *We always/usually/___ spent . . .* • *On Sundays we ___ often . . .* • *I had never . . .*
Specific event	• *One time/But ___ night/ On this occasion . . .* • *The problem was that . . .*
Reflecting	• *Looking back, . . .* • *It's ___ to believe* • *I can hardly believe . . .*

Speaking

11a Choose two or three childhood memories or experiences to talk about. Write a few notes and try to use some of the expressions in the How To box.

b **Group Work** Share your stories. Ask questions about your classmates' stories.

Writing

12 Write a paragraph describing an early childhood memory, using phrases from the How To box.

Extra Vocabulary Study and Extra Listening Activity in ACTIVEBOOK

Review

1 Rewrite each sentence so that the meaning stays the same. Use the words in bold.

1. It won't be a surprise if the manager is angry about the situation. **likely**
2. I'm sure they'll call us this morning. **bound**
3. They asked me to be there at 10:30. **supposed**
4. There must be another way out of the building. **can't**
5. Maybe we'll have time to chat before the meeting. **might**
6. They are refusing to pay the bill until the dispute has been resolved. **won't**
7. Do you want us to wait for you outside the conference hall? **should**
8. It's better if he brings his own laptop. **ought**

2 Complete each sentence with a suitable modal phrase in the past.

Ex: The mud was up to 16 feet (5 meters) deep in places.
It *must have been* impossible to drive through.

1. Why isn't she here? She __________ understood your instructions.
2. You should have seen their reaction! They __________ been happier.
3. We were lucky to get out alive. We __________ killed.
4. They didn't come home until the early hours of the morning. The party __________ good.
5. She could see my face. She __________ realized who I was.
6. They'd had such a difficult journey. They __________ relieved when they arrived.
7. They lost the game. Sam __________ disappointed.

3 Correct any mistakes in the sentences. Not all sentences have mistakes.

1. If I'd have known, I'd have called you earlier.
2. I wish she won't always tell me what to do.
3. I wouldn't change it for the world.
4. We left the keys in the office so you will see them when you got there.
5. I'd sit on my grandfather's knee and put tobacco in his pipe.
6. Wouldn't it be easier if we went home first?
7. I told Marcella that we meet her outside the theater.
8. My parents wouldn't never have dreamed of sending me to private school.

4 Complete the paragraph with words from the box.

end	calm	aback	pleased	terrified	delighted
tends	minds	upset	thrilled	worked	

When I was about ten years old, I remember my father coming into the room, looking very __________ (1.) with himself, to tell us that we were going to have another brother or sister. It was unexpected, so we were both taken __________ (2.), but I was __________ (3.). My brother, on the other hand, was of two __________ (4.). He was younger than me, and I don't think he was too impressed with the idea. He __________ (5.) to worry about things, and I think he was __________ (6.) by the fact that he might not be the center of attention all the time. When the big day came, unfortunately there were problems, and my mother had to stay in the hospital. We weren't allowed to visit, and we were all at our wits __________ (7.) with worry. We tried to __________ (8.) each other down, but basically we were all __________ (9.) that something awful would happen. It all __________ (10.) out in the end though, and when I was finally able to see my little sister, I was __________ (11.). She was so tiny and special. We all love her so much.

Communication | express strong feelings about an issue

5 Read the dictionary definitions and discuss. When was the last time you complained about something, raved about something, or took a stand on something?

complain /kəm'pleɪn/ *v* [I] **1** *informal* to say that you are annoyed, not satisfied, or unhappy about something or someone

take a stand *v* [I] to state publicly a strong opinion about an important issue

rave /reɪv/ *v* [I] **1 rave about/over something** to talk in an excited way about something because you think it is very good

6 2.20 Listen to the speakers. What does each speaker talk about? Are they complaining about something, raving about something, or taking a stand? What are their opinions?

7 Think about an issue or topic that you feel strongly about. Prepare to explain your feelings. Use the pictures below if you need inspiration.

8 **Group Work** Explain your position. As you are listening to other students, write down their topics and one question to ask when they have finished.

Unit 6 Reference

Articles

Definite article

Classes: *The arctic fox is known to inhabit the area.*

National groups: *The French are unhappy about the new policy.*

Other groups: *The Green Party has staged a protest.*

Unique objects: *The sun was setting on the horizon.*

Titles: *The president has yet to make a decision.*

Musical instruments: *She learned to play the harp.*

Geographical names: rivers (*the Amazon*), oceans (*the Pacific*), compass points (*the North Pole*), collective countries (*the EU*), mountain ranges (*the Alps*). NOT: lakes (~~*the Lake Erie*~~), single mountains (~~*the Mount Everest*~~), continents (~~*the Asia*~~)

Shared knowledge or experience: *We'll meet them in the café.* (the café by our office—shared knowledge)

Indefinite article

Jobs: *Martha is a dentist.*

Measuring: *It costs $150 a week. (per week)*

Introducing something new: *There's been an accident!*

No article

Names: *Tom Cruise is my favorite actor.*

Streets: *They live on Harvard Street.*

General countable plurals: *I love cats.* NOT: ~~*I love the cats.*~~

Clauses with *whatever, whoever, whenever*

Use *whenever, whatever, whoever*, etc. when it doesn't make any difference *when, what, who*, etc., or we don't have to be specific, OR we don't know the exact details of *when, what, who*, etc.

*Come **whenever** you can.* (It doesn't matter exactly when you come)

What, who, and *when* are a little different from *whatever, whoever*, and *whenever*. Compare:

*Repeat **what** you just said!* ✓

*Repeat **whatever** you just said!* ✓

***Whatever** you just said, repeat it!* ✓

NOT: ~~*What you just said, repeat it!*~~ ✗

***Whoever** you saw was probably the criminal.* ✓

NOT: ~~*Who you saw was probably the criminal.*~~ ✗

However has two meanings. Compare:

***However** you go, by train or by car, it takes a day.*

*It takes two days by car. **However,** if you go by train, it takes only a day.* (contrast)

Connectors of time and contrast

There are many words and expressions that allow us to link our ideas and narratives in different ways.

To link things happening at the same time: *while, when, as, during*

***As** the plane took off, she felt free.*

To link things that happen when other longer actions are finishing or have finished: *by which time, at which point.*

*I reached the end, **by which time** I was tired.*

To link things that happen immediately after the previous action: *hardly* + *when*, *on* + present participle, *no sooner* + *than*

***On hearing** of the crash, he ran straight to the hospital.*

To link things that contrast with previous information: *though, although,* and *even though* + verb phrase

***Although he's short,** he's good at basketball.*

We can also use *despite* and *in spite of* + noun phrase or gerund.

***In spite of my poor grades,** I got a good job.*

We can use adjective/adverb + *as/though* + subject + verb to add emphasis to the contrast. Typical examples are *much as* (*I like*), *hard though* (*we tried*).

***Much as I love** television, even I can't watch for more than three or four hours a day.*

Unit Vocabulary

Power

win over	be impressed by
gain	play an important part

Fashions and fads

catch on	be out	home in on
come about	be in	keep up with

Personal characteristics

inspirational	charismatic	dignified
nondescript	idealistic	tireless
gravitas	approachable	resolute
down-to-earth	trustworthy	inspiring
drive or energy	corrupt	aloof
waver in the face of problems		

Unit 7 Reference

Adjective clauses

Restrictive adjective clauses make it clear who or what is being referred to. They cannot be omitted.

That's the town ***where*** *I lived ten years ago.*

That can replace *who* or *which*.

They're playing the song ***which*** *Jenny wrote =*
They're playing the song ***that*** *Jenny wrote.*

If the relative pronoun is the object of the clause, it can be omitted.

John ate the cake ***(that/which)*** *we bought yesterday.*

Don't use commas before the relative pronoun in restrictive adjective clauses.

Non-restrictive adjective clauses give extra information. This information can be omitted.

I went rock climbing last weekend, ***which was fun.***

That cannot replace *who* or *which*.

The relative pronoun cannot be omitted.

Use a comma before and after non-restrictive adjective clauses, unless they end the sentence.

Adjective clauses with verb + dependent preposition usually have the preposition at the end of the clause.

That's the company (which) I worked ***for.***

In formal English, put the preposition at the beginning of the clause.

That's the company ***for which*** *I worked.*

A common pattern is (*one/some/all/either/neither*, etc.) *of which/whom*. This pattern is slightly formal.

I saw two women, ***neither of whom*** *was tall.*

Verbs followed by infinitives or gerunds

Some verbs can be followed by the infinitive or the gerund. Sometimes the meaning changes.

Going there ***means*** *entering a new world.* = involves
I ***didn't mean*** *to break the door.* = didn't intend

Some verbs of perception (*hear, watch, feel, observe*, etc.) don't change their meaning when followed by different verb forms. BUT compare:

a. *I* ***saw the camel eat*** *the leaves.*
b. *I* ***saw the camel eating*** *the leaves.*

Sentence **a** describes a finished action. Sentence **b** describes an action that may be unfinished.

As . . . as; describing quantity

Use *as . . . as* to say that two things are equal in some way.

As . . . as can be used with adjectives, adverbs, *much* and *many*.

I'm ***as strong as*** *an ox.*
He sang ***as sweetly as*** *an angel.*
The motorcycle costs ***as much as*** *a car.*

A clause can be put after the second *as*.

She doesn't talk to me ***as much as she used to.***

Possible, *ever*, or *usual* is often placed after the second *as*.

I got here as quickly ***as possible.***
You're looking as beautiful ***as ever.***
The program wasn't as interesting ***as usual.***

Unit Vocabulary

Animals and their environment

endangered	sanctuary	cage
animal rights	mammal	reptile
animal testing	carnivore	fur trade
nature preserve	predator	exotic
over-hunting/fishing		

Descriptive language

active volcano	permanent settlement
ghost town	spectacular landscape
below sea level	tourist destination

drenched	zig-zag	loom
trespass	warped	drone
hunched	vibrant	parched

Buying and selling

It's in excellent condition.	It's as good as new.
It's the latest model.	It's state of the art.
It's second hand.	It's used.
It's available now.	It's on the market.
It's hand crafted.	It's brand new.
It's made by hand.	It includes ____
It's still in its packaging.	It features ____
It's one of a kind.	It's unique.

It has some wear and tear.
It comes in a wide range of ____.
You can choose from a selection of ____.
It's not in perfect condition.

Unit 8 Reference

Reporting verbs

Reporting verbs show the function of the original piece of speech.

"You can't leave the office before 6:00." → *She informed him that he couldn't leave the office before 6:00.*

Reporting verbs use different patterns. The majority use a verb + (*that*) clause. Other examples are:

Verb + *that* clause: *accept, recollect, respond, imply, insist, presume, maintain, suggest, answer, confess, remember, conclude, state, boast, repeat*

Verb + object + infinitive: *persuade, remind, tell, advise, urge, warn, expect, force, invite, order*

Verb + object + *that* clause: *inform, advise, remind, tell, warn*

Verb + infinitive: *agree, refuse, propose, decide*

Verb + gerund: *deny, regret, suggest, mention*

Verb + object + preposition + present participle: *blame* (someone) *for, congratulate* (someone) *on, thank* (someone) *for*

Continuous forms

Use continuous tenses to talk about:

- background actions that are in progress at the moment we describe:
  *When I woke up, **it was raining**.*
- actions that are temporary or incomplete:
  *She**'s working** for me right now.*
- actions that are repeated:
  ***I've been training** every day for the last month.*
- actions in the process of change:
  *Prices **are rising**.*
- Stative verbs are not usually used in the continuous. Some common stative verbs are:
- Verbs of personal feeling: *like, love, hate, want, prefer, dislike, wish*
- Verbs of thought: *know, believe, imagine, mean, realize, understand, doubt, feel* (have an opinion)
- Verbs of the senses: *hear, sound, appear, taste, see, smell, resemble, seem*
- Verbs of fixed situations: *depend on, contain, belong to, own, involve, include, possess*

Some stative verbs have a progressive form, but the meaning may be a little different.

*I **feel** he should win.* (belief) ***I'm feeling** sick.* (sense)

*I **see** your point.* (understand) ***I'm seeing** the boss tomorrow.* (plan to meet)

Fronting

Sometimes in informal English a sentence begins with the complement (object, verb, adjective, or adverb). This gives the complement more emphasis.

Intelligent she may be, but kind she isn't!

What or another question word is sometimes used.

I don't know what she's doing here! → ***What** she's doing here I don't know!*

I'll never understand why you went there. → ***Why** you went there I'll never understand.*

Fronting can be used to provide a link to information already mentioned.

*Her first book was bad. **Much better was her second.***

We can front verbs and adjectives with *as* and ***though***.

***Tired though I was,** I didn't stop running.*

There are a number of common fronting phrases that show the importance of what follows.

***The trouble is,** he's so lazy.*

***The question is,** can we get her to join us?*

***The fact of the matter is,** you're not strong enough.*

***The fact remains** that we still have no definite date.*

Unit Vocabulary

Global issues

multiculturalism, giant corporations, cost and safety issues, cloning, pollution, identity theft, global warming, oil spill, energy

Positive and negative opinions

It's a waste of space. / We can do without it. / We can't do without it. / It's been disastrous. / It's overrated. / It's underrated. / It's indispensable. / It's had big benefits.

Lifestyles

tear my hair out, a security blanket, burn out, the be-all and end-all, the buzz

Cause and effect

consequence, has its origins in, an influence on, bring about, give rise to, a major source of, stem from, result in

Unit 9 Reference

Collocations with prepositions

Sometimes verbs are followed by a preposition: *ask for, contribute to, range from . . . (to . . .), suffer from*

The verb and preposition are sometimes separated by the object: *remind someone of, distinguish someone from, receive training in*

Sometimes nouns are followed by prepositions: *relationship with, insurance against, in the fields of*

Sometimes adjectives are followed by a preposition: *bad at, similar to, famous for, concerned about*

Sometimes prepositions can begin common phrases: *in advance, out of order, at the time, on one occasion*

Discourse markers

Discourse is a piece of language that is longer and more complex than a sentence.

We use **discourse markers** to organize our speech or writing and make clear the relationship between what we have said and what we will say. We also use discourse markers to show our attitude toward a subject. The use of discourse markers depends on the function of our speech. For example, persuading, agreeing, etc., use different markers.

Here are some common discourse markers:

- focusing on the main topic: *regarding, as far as ___ is concerned, as for*
- returning to the main point (what was said before didn't matter): *anyway, anyhow, at any rate*
- returning to a previous line of discussion: *as I was saying, anyway, what I was going to say was*
- introducing a strong opinion or criticism: *all the same, and yet, still, on the other hand*

Unreal past

Wish or *If only*

Use *wish* or *if only* to describe unreal or imaginary situations. These are often regrets.

Wish or *If only* + past tenses describe imaginary present or future: ***If only** I **were** stronger.*

Wish or *If only* + past perfect describes the imaginary past: *I **wish** I **had bought** that CD.*

Wish + object + *would* is used to complain: *I **wish** you **would be** quiet!*

It's time, It's high time, It's about time

Use *it's time*, etc. + past tenses to say something should be happening now but isn't. It is often used for criticizing someone or something.

*It's **high time** you **stopped** acting like a child.*

Would rather

Use *would rather* + simple past to describe preferences: ***I'd rather** she **gave** me the cash.*

If the person who expresses the preference and the subject are the same, use *would rather* + base form. ***I'd rather dance** the tango than the foxtrot.*

These expressions are often used to refuse permission: ***I'd rather** you **didn't smoke** in my home.*

What if or *Suppose*

Use *what if* or *suppose* + past tenses to ask about an imaginary situation in the present or future:

***Suppose** you **asked** the bank for a loan?*

Use *what if* or *suppose* + past perfect to ask about an imaginary situation in the past:

***What if** we **had arrived** earlier?*

Use *what if* or *suppose* + simple present to ask about a situation that you think is probable:

***What if** your plan **doesn't work**?*

Unit Vocabulary

Describing art

It's not my kind of thing.	abstract
It's not my taste.	avant-garde
I can't relate to it.	traditional
It's not my cup of tea.	contemporary
I'm a big fan of his stuff.	art deco
I'm really into her work.	disturbing
I've always admired her work.	tranquil
He's one of my all-time favorites.	figurative
his/her finest piece	striking
not one of his best	dull
masterpiece	stereotyped
over the top	poor acting
breathtaking	disappointing
fantastic/difficult/heavy read	spectacular

Unit 10 Reference

Modals (and verbs with similar meanings)

don't have to
lack of obligation: *We **don't have to go** until 2:30.*

must not
obligation not to do something: *You **mustn't talk** to him like that.*

should or ***ought to***
advice: *You **should see** a doctor.*

recommendation: *You **ought to see** the castle.*

polite obligation: *Guests **should not smoke** in the bedrooms.*

uncertainty: ***Should** we **lock** both the doors?*

expectation: *They **should be** here by now.*

can
permission: ***Can** I **use** the telephone?*

can't
impossibility: *This **can't be** the right place!*

can + be
criticism: *He **can be** so annoying!*

will
assumption: *They**'ll be** here in a minute.*

won't
refusal: *I **won't stop** until I get what I want.*

may or ***might***
possibility: *We **might need** an umbrella.*

might as well
the last option, when the speaker is not enthusiastic: *We **might as well just pay** the bill.*

must
certainty: *They **must be** hungry by now.*

need
behaves like a normal verb: ***Do** you **need to speak** to the doctor?*

is supposed to
obligation: *They **were supposed to deliver** the package this morning.*

be bound to
prediction of certainty: *He**'s bound to get** the job.*

be likely to do or ***be***
probability: *Children living in rural areas **are likely to move** to the city as adults.*

Modals of deduction (past)

must have (been)
certain: *The crash **must have been** terrifying.*

might have (been)
possibility: *I **might have left** my keys in the car.*

can't have or ***couldn't have (been)***
impossibility: *He **can't have finished** already! They **couldn't have come** this far.*

could have or ***may have (been)***
possibility: *We **could have been** left there for a long time. There **may have been** a good reason for the delay, but we were angry anyway.*

Uses of *would*

polite request: ***Would** you help me get the files?*

recurring situation in the past: *She **would** always have a pack of gum in her pocket.*

past purpose or reason (often used after *so that*): *We took a taxi so (that) we **wouldn't** be late.*

imagined situation: ***I'd** love to know what happened!*

strong wish that someone would or wouldn't do something: *I wish he **would** make more of an effort!*

past intention or expectation (reported): *They asked if we **would** like anything to drink.*

past refusal: *He **wouldn't** let go of my bag.*

Unit Vocabulary

Idioms and phrases for feelings

down in the dumps	at her wits end
kicking themselves	of two minds
pleased with herself	wound up

Outlook and attitude

tend to trust	go through
look on the bright side	dwell on things
work out in the long run	chances are

Strong feelings

thrilled	outraged	taken aback
ecstatic	indifferent	miserable
upset	terrified	flabbergasted
furious	delighted	dumbstruck
livid	petrified	uninterested

Speaking Exchange

Unit 9 | Page 110, Exercise 3a

Student A

On Being a Travel Photographer

A picture is worth a thousand words—but only if it's good.

Introduction

Imagine this: early morning, the sun rising over the Swiss Alps, light glistening off fresh snow, flowers opening to greet the dawn. The scene is incredibly beautiful, and you wish you could capture the image forever. So you take a picture.

Unfortunately, on returning home, you find that the photo is blurred at the edges, and your finger takes up half the frame. "If only I'd taken a better picture!" you cry. "I wish I had a decent camera!" Actually, it's not about the camera. If you really want a good photographic record of your trip, it's high time you learned a few basics.

1. Composition

Suppose you see a beautiful landscape stretching in front of you for miles. What do you do? Don't try to fit it all in. Pick one interesting part and focus on it. Look for natural lines that draw the viewer in and give your picture depth, like a river starting in the foreground and disappearing into the distance.

2. Time of day

If traveling, the best time of day for a photo is either early morning or late afternoon. The light is softer at these times of day, unlike midday light, which can be too harsh for some subject matter. Make sure to keep the sun behind you, or you may end up with a silhouette of your intended subject. If you're shooting at night, keep your subjects no farther than 8–10 feet (3 meters) away; even the strongest flash can't illuminate more space.

3. Focus

What if you want a close-up of a person or animal? What do you focus on? The eyes. The most interesting travel photography often includes people or animals as well as beautiful environments. And much can be conveyed through people's eyes. Get as close as possible and fill the frame. There should be nothing in the picture that doesn't relate to the subject. Also, look for symmetrical subjects; it doesn't have to be a mirror image, just well-balanced.

4. Learn from others

Keep your eyes open; be aware of your surroundings. Before traveling, spend some time looking through big coffee-table picture books and magazines to see how the professionals do it. Take note of different ways in which light, perspective, and color are used. And don't be afraid to experiment: change the angle, get on your knees, climb onto a chair, find a balcony with a view.

5. Be sensitive

In many cultures, the people would rather you asked before photographing them. Take time to get to know them. Learn a few words of the language so that you can be polite. They are more likely to smile if you have addressed them in their language.

Unit 7 | Page 90, Exercise 8

Student A

You want to build a luxury hotel with a golf course. The hotel could also serve as a conference center. It will bring lots of money and jobs to the local economy, and encourage businesses such as tourist shops, tour guides, and new restaurants.

Unit 8 | Page 99, Exercise 5

Student C

Your friend is an Internet addict. She spends up to seven hours a day online. You want to help her, but you are worried that she will be offended.

Unit 10 | Page 117, Exercise 6b

HOW OPTIMISTIC ARE YOU?

Add up your total score from the questionnaire on page 119. Then find your optimism rating below:

48–60: You are definitely a "glass-half-full" type of person—an eternal optimist. Almost nothing can make you feel bad. You greet life head-on, convinced that you cannot fail. And chances are that you will succeed a great deal of the time. However, it's important to take a minute every now and then to make sure that you are not being unrealistically optimistic.

30–47: You may have found a happy medium between optimism and pessimism. You know that it's important to have a positive outlook on life while at the same time being realistic about what you can and cannot achieve. If you are at the lower end of this spectrum, you may want to remember to try to ignore those negative thoughts when they begin to be more numerous than the positive ones.

12–29: Like many of us, you may think of yourself as a realist. Take care, however, not to let negative thought patterns rule your life. You may want to try cognitive restructuring—when you are aware of a negative thought, consciously replace it with a positive one. When something good happens in your life, realize that you are responsible for it, and don't assume that everything bad that happens is your fault.

Unit 8 | Page 99, Exercise 5

Student A

Your friend works too hard. He has a tough job and spends all of his time at work. He doesn't look healthy, and he isn't much fun to be with. You want to help him, but you are worried he will reject your advice.

Unit 10 | Page 119, Exercise 6b

Picture 1
Polo player Peter Koscinsky feels the pain after falling off his horse. It happened when he was attacking the ball and collided with an opposing team player. To make matters worse, the umpire awarded a free goal to the other side, which meant his team lost.

Picture 2
Chimpsky is on a beach, being filmed for a soft drink ad. Apparently, the three-and-a-half-year-old chimpanzee enjoyed the drink so much that he finished four bottles and had to be excused for numerous bathroom breaks.

Picture 3
Stuntman Todd Carter does his stuff for a forthcoming film about tornadoes. The truck, which is made of a very light metal and has no engine, was lifted into the tree by a crane, with Carter in it!

Picture 4
Actor Jack Black was the voice for the hero Po in the animated movie *Kung Fu Panda*, and Dustin Hoffman was the voice for his "co-star," Shifu. Here they goof off at the Berlin premiere of the movie.

Unit 7 | Page 90, Exercise 8

Student C

You want to start an alternative community for a maximum of 50 people. The residents will farm the land, growing all their own food and living in harmony with nature. Throughout the year there will be music festivals, as well as regular yoga, tai chi, and a school for children.

Student B

On Being a Travel Writer

Introduction

Moving out of the shade of the high palm trees, you stroll for one last time along the sand dunes, allowing the transparent water to brush over your feet. You head for the bar, sip slowly on a cocktail, go to your beachfront hotel suite, and write 600 words. You email it the following morning to the travel magazine, before checking out with the immortal line, "Put the bill on my company's expense account."

"Ah, if only I were a travel writer!" you say. "I wish I could live like that!" Unfortunately, being a travel writer is no picnic.

1. Write often

The way to become a better writer is to write regularly. Some people say they don't have time. This isn't true. You have to *make time*. Start by keeping a journal every day. It doesn't matter what time of day you write it as long as you do it. Use it to record sights, sounds, smells, tastes. If you've always wanted to write, it's about time you started—no excuses.

2. Travel with your senses

Suppose you could have either a week on a beach or a week exploring a hot, dangerous jungle. Which would you choose? Travel writers would rather go to the jungle. Don't be a tourist; be a traveler. Keep your eyes and ears open for unusual details. Professional travel writers don't just see the normal things (the pretty sunset); they spot things that most tourists don't see (the sound of a bat's wings, the way a boat leans in the wind). Learn from them. And interact with the local culture: talk to people, try the food, haggle in the markets. You can't write well about something unless you really understand it.

3. Look for a story

Like journalists, travel writers look for stories, not just descriptions. Find something unusual that has happened and ask why it happened and what the consequences were. Look for a beginning, a middle, and an ending. Alternatively, find an original angle. Thousands upon thousands of people have written about the Grand Canyon, but what if you could interview someone who lived in it, or parachuted into it, or got lost in it . . .?

4. No cash, but a strong stomach

Only a tiny minority of travel writers get paid to do it, and it's rarely enough money to live on. You need a combination of talent, luck, and perseverance. Oh, and a strong stomach. Who knows what you'll have to eat in the name of research?

Unit 10 | Page 119, Exercise 6a

Unit 7 | Page 90, Exercise 8

Student B

You want to have a wildlife sanctuary. You believe there needs to be a place where wild animals are protected. You think it's fine for some paying customers to come and view the wildlife, but you don't want too many tourists to spoil the atmosphere. You will bring in a lot of wildlife for the sanctuary.

Unit 8 | Page 99, Exercise 5

Student B

You regularly go to the gym with a friend, but he spends the whole time chatting, not exercising. You don't want to go with him any more, but you are afraid of hurting his feelings.

Writing Bank

Unit 6 | Page 76, Exercise 9a

Autobiographical statements

1 Read the autobiographical statement. Which summary is the most accurate?

a. The writer is applying for a job at a design company.

b. The writer is explaining how she became a graphic designer.

c. The writer is trying to enroll in an academic program.

I was born in Miami, but I grew up in Reed City, which is a small town with not much to do, so my two sisters and I had to improvise and invent a lot of games. This is probably one reason I was good at making things. As a child, I always enjoyed designing objects to put in rooms, and my teachers encouraged me to develop my artistic abilities. I also found that I had a particular aptitude for math.

At the age of 18 I began an apprenticeship with a design company. I worked for Bilosh Design Solutions for two years, mainly doing clerical work in the office, but also observing some of the projects. During this time I learned a lot, especially from Judith Baker, who was my manager. She taught me how to solve problems by looking at things in a different way. From her I learned how to "think outside the box."

In 2011 I felt that I needed a new challenge, so I decided to enroll in a cartoon animation course. I spent a very enjoyable month working on film animation. It was at this time that I realized that my true vocation was designing graphics for advertisements and commercial films. For this reason, I have applied to the School for Design graphic design program. I hope to develop my skills so that I will be able to work in this field for the foreseeable future.

Cheryl Nemeth

Writing skill | redrafting

2 Here are some sentences and phrases that Cheryl wrote originally and then changed. Which sentences and phrases did she replace them with? Why are the rewritten sentences and phrases better (think about formal vs. informal, style, economy of words, repetition)?

Example: *"the town is incredibly boring"* she rewrote *"which is a small town with not much to do."* She changed this because the first version sounds too negative.

1. I always enjoyed designing things
2. I was also really good at math
3. doing tasks like photocopying, sending faxes, mailing letters and ordering materials
4. I'd had enough of Bilosh
5. I will be able to work in graphic design

Useful Phrases

Organizing time and sequence	• *as a child,* • *at the age of . . .* • *during this time,* • *I spent a month/year . . .* • *it was at this time that . . .* • *. . . for the foreseeable future*
Explaining stages in your career path	• *had an aptitude for . . .* • *began an apprenticeship* • *enroll in a program* • *apply to a program* • *my true vocation*

Unit 8 | Page 100, Exercise 10a

Cause and effect essays

1 Read the essay. Which title best fits the essay?

a. Insomnia—Causes and Effects

b. How Stress Affects Your Sleep

c. Five Ideas for a Better Sleep

It has been estimated that around 90 percent of adults in the developed world have, at some time in their life, suffered from a period of insomnia of at least one week. Other recent research has shown that women are nearly twice as likely as men to have it. There are a number of causes, which can be roughly put into three categories: lifestyle, environment, and health.

Lifestyle greatly affects the way we sleep. People who smoke or drink alcohol and coffee (or other drinks with caffeine) close to bedtime are more vulnerable to insomnia. Another aspect of lifestyle that affects our sleep is physical activity. People who exercise are more likely to sleep soundly than those who do no physical exercise. Also, those who work in highly stressful jobs, under a lot of pressure, often have trouble "turning off" and relaxing, and this affects the quality and quantity of their sleep.

The second cause is environment. Bedrooms should be quiet, dark, and cool. Furthermore, they should not be used as an office or a place of work. Instead, the bedroom should be a retreat from our daily activities. While many people report that they get used to living in noisy neighborhoods, for others silence is essential for a good night's sleep.

The third cause of insomnia is health. Both physical and mental health affect the way we sleep. Pain, illness, and an unhealthy diet leading to excess body fat can all cause insomnia. Regarding mental health, any stressful situation causing emotions such as fear, panic, and nervousness may keep us from sleeping.

So what are the effects of insomnia? Many insomniacs report feeling drowsy during the day. This prevents them from learning, recalling information, and concentrating to their full capacity. One potentially dangerous side effect of this may occur when they are handling machinery. A large number of car accidents take place because of the effects of insomnia.

A further effect is irritability. Insomniacs may experience mood swings during which they feel angry for no reason, while long-term lack of sleep may lead to depression. For this reason, people who are living with the insomniac need to be aware of the effects.

Writing skill | reference words

2 What do these words refer to?

1. *it* (line 6)
   a. sleep b. a partner who suffers from insomnia
   c. insomnia
2. *those* (line 14)
   a. people b. exercises c. types of drink
3. *they* (line 20)
   a. environments b. people c. bedrooms
4. *this* (line 35)
   a. insomnia b. feeling drowsy c. the day
5. *they* (line 42)
   a. feelings of depression b. insomniacs
   c. mood swings

Useful Phrases

Text organization	• *The second . . .* • *The third . . .*
Adding information	• *Another* (aspect) • *Also* • *Furthermore* • *A further* (effect)
Referring	• *Regarding* • *For this reason*

Phrasal Verbs

A phrasal verb consists of two or more words: a verb + a particle (an adverb or a preposition) [+ a preposition]. The meaning of a phrasal verb is usually very different from the meaning of the verb alone. For example, the phrasal verbs *look up* (search for in a book or other source) and *look after* (care for) have very different meanings from *look*.

Some phrasal verbs are intransitive, (they cannot take an object). The majority are transitive (they take an object). Sometimes the object can come after the particle or after the verb. For example, hand in your papers / hand your papers in / hand them in. These phrasal verbs are known as *separable*. With other phrasal verbs the words in the phrase cannot be separated; they are known as *inseparable*.

Some common phrasal verbs

Separable	
Ask out	ask someone on a date
Bring up	1) raise children 2) mention a subject
Call back	return a phone call
Call off	cancel
Call up	make a phone call
Figure out	find the solution
Fill in	give detailed information
Fill out	writing information on a form
Fill up	fill completely
Give back	return
Hand out	give to each person in a group; distribute
Hold up	keep waiting
Look over	examine carefully
Look up	search for information in a book or other source
Make up	Invent (a story)
Pick up	1) lift 2) collect in a car
Put away	put something where it belongs
Put back	return to the place it was found
Put off	Delay doing something you don't want to do; procrastinate
Shut off	turn off; stop
Show up	make someone feel stupid or bad
Split up	to end a relationship
Take back	return
Tear down	destroy
Try on	put something on to check the fit
Turn around	change direction
Turn down	refuse
Turn in	1) produce a great result 2) tell the police about a criminal 3) go to bed
Turn up	increase the volume
Work out	resolve a problem

Inseparable	
Catch on	1) understand 2) become popular
Come across	find by chance
Come by	visit
Come from	born in a place; originate
Come up with	invent or create something
Cut back/down on	use less; reduce
Fit in	be accepted by others
Get along with	have a friendly relationship
Get away from	escape
Get away with	go unnoticed or unpunished
Get in	enter
Get over	recover
Get up	get out of bed
Give up	stop trying
Go on	1) continue 2) happen
Go for	choose
Go through	1) experience 2) spend 3) check 4) be approved
Grow up	become an adult
Hang up	end a phone conversation
Keep out of	stay away from; not be involved
Make off with	steal
Make up	apologize after a quarrel
Look into	investigate
Look forward to	anticipate
Look up to	admire
Put up with	tolerate
See to	deal with someone or something
Take after	look or behave like a relative
Turn up	appear suddenly
Work out	exercise

Audioscript

UNIT 6 Understanding power

1.28 (Page 69)

A: "La Tour Eiffel" in Paris was built in 1889 to commemorate the 100th anniversary of the French Revolution. The Industrial Revolution in Europe had brought about a new trend—the use of metal in construction. The tower, built from a lattice made from very pure iron, is light and able to withstand high wind pressures. For 40 years from the time that it was built, it stood as the tallest tower in the world, and today it is still the tallest building in Paris.

B: The Pentagon, covering 34 acres, is thought to be the largest office building in the world. It takes a person fifteen to twenty minutes to walk around the building once. It was built in five concentric rings, in record time during the Second World War, in order to relocate employees of the War Department from the seventeen buildings they occupied within Washington D.C.

A: Built between 1406 and 1420 during the Ming dynasty, The Forbidden City, also called the Purple Forbidden City, or Gugong Museum in Chinese, is located in the center of Beijing. Occupying a rectangular area of more than 720,000 square meters, the Forbidden City was the imperial home of twenty-four emperors of the Ming (1368–1644) and Qing (1644–1911) dynasties. It is one of the largest and best-preserved palace complexes in the world, with over a million rare and valuable objects in the museum.

B: The CN Tower, a communications and observation tower in Toronto, Canada, was named for Canadian National, the railway company that built it. Completed in 1976, the 553-meter CN Tower was the world's tallest tower for 34 years. It remains the tallest free-standing structure in the Western Hemisphere and attracts more than two million visitors each year. From its Sky Pod, which is the second-highest public observation deck in the world, it is possible to see up to 120 kilometers away, to the mist rising from Niagara Falls.

A: The Great Pyramid is arguably the most accomplished engineering feat of the Ancient World. Built to house the body of the dead pharaoh, the base of the Great Pyramid in Egypt is 230 meters square, large enough to cover ten football fields. According to the Greek historian Herodotus, it took 400,000 men twenty years to construct this great monument. They used 2.3 million blocks of stone, some of which weighed as much as 50 tons!

B: Chan Chan, the largest adobe city in the Americas, was built about 1200 years ago in what is now northern Peru. It was the capital of the Chimu civilization, which lasted from A.D. 850 to around 1470. Chan Chan consisted of 10,000 structures, some with walls as high as 9 meters—including the huge, elaborately decorated palaces of the Chimu kings. The city covered 20 square kilometers and, though it was built on a coastal desert, boasted a sophisticated network of irrigation canals and wells. Efforts are currently underway to preserve Chan Chan, which is threatened with erosion by increased rainfall in recent years.

A: The Sydney Harbor Bridge is one of Australia's best known, and most photographed landmarks. It is the world's largest (but not the longest) steel arch bridge with the top of the bridge standing 134 meters above the harbor. Fondly known by the Australians as the "coathanger," Sydney Harbor Bridge celebrated its 70th birthday in 2002. Nowadays, a group of twelve people leave every ten minutes to climb to the top of the bridge and admire spectacular views of the city, and out to the Tasman Sea.

1.29 (Page 71)

A: I think, with technology, it was Microsoft that started it.

B: "It" being the use of teenagers . . .

A: Using teenagers to find out what's in and what isn't, what the market wants next. Around the year 2000, they started observing kids to find out what they were doing with technology. They went all over the place observing kids: from street markets in Seattle to skating rinks in London, bars in Tokyo, anywhere they thought trends might start.

B: So the idea was to watch teenagers, and learn what they wanted to do with their cell phones, with software . . .

A: That's right. Because it's teenagers that really drive technology. Kids have no fear of technology. They experiment, and they automatically home in on the new. One thing that became clear is that teenagers want technology they can carry around. Anything bigger than a few inches is out.

B: And now we have tiny phones and tablets that are practically computers—they do almost everything.

A: Yup. Text messaging caught on because kids wanted to pass notes to each other during class. And now texting is almost more popular than actual face-to-face talking. What else . . . the lights that you find on keyboards are there because tech companies noticed that kids take notes in the dark during lectures.

B: So all of these things came about because of the needs of kids.

A: That's right. And don't forget about Facebook—it was developed first as a way for college students to share information. And now it, along with Twitter, has revolutionized the way almost the entire world communicates.

B: So is it just technology with these kids?

A: You mean where teenagers are leading the market?

B: Yes.

A: Not at all. I mean, fashion has been youth-led for years and years, but in particular, sneakers. Now, if you want to keep up with the latest style, who do you ask? You don't ask anyone over twenty, that's for sure. And I think it was Converse who used to do lots of their market research on the streets, on the basketball courts of New York, anywhere you find teenagers. They may still do it, I don't know.

B: And, what, they just talk to these kids?

A: Talk to them, watch what they are wearing, the colors, the styles, and maybe bring in a prototype, ask the kids if they'd wear them. If not, why not?

1.30 (Page 72)

Conversation 1

A: Well, it depends on the age.

B: I agree.

A: When they're young teenagers, no I don't think so.

B: What kind of limits would you put on, say, a fifteen year old?

A: It depends. There are some places that are not OK for teenagers.

B: Such as?

A: I wouldn't let my fifteen-year-old go to a bar, for instance.

Conversation 2

C: Teenagers? I don't think so.

D: Really? Why not?

C: Because . . .well, I think there are still things that they shouldn't see, that are inappropriate. Plus, they could be doing other things.

D: It's not that good for their eyes either, is it?

Conversation 3

E: Oh, definitely, yeah. They're our friends.

F: Me too. If parents can choose who they hang out with, then we should too.

E: What's the difference?

F: Exactly. It's not like we're stupid and can't judge someone's character.

Conversation 4

G: I think if it's a school day the next day, then it makes sense to have some kind of limit.

H: Yeah, but who sets the limit? If you know you're going to be OK on six hours' sleep or something . . .

G: Yeah, you should discuss it, but if you're going to be exhausted in the morning then that's not really . . .

H: I'm saying it's not up to the parents to decide. We're old enough—we know how to turn off the lights, don't we?

1.31 (Page 73)

Example

A: Whatever you do, don't forget to turn off the power.

1

B: Whenever you feel down, give me a call.

2

A: Wherever we go, they're always close behind.

3

B: Whenever I can, I'll see her.

4

A: Whoever we hire, he'll have to work miracles.

5

B: Whatever those children do, they make a success of it.

1.32 (Page 76)

1. She's very charismatic.
2. I find him inspirational.

3. He's very dignified.
4. She's pretty aloof.
5. He's so idealistic.
6. They are tireless.
7. He's not very trustworthy.
8. She's extremely resolute.

A. She doesn't have much drive or energy.
B. He wavers in the face of problems.
C. He's very approachable.
D. He's corrupt.
E. She's fairly nondescript.
F. She's very down-to-earth and practical.
G. She's not very inspiring.
H. She lacks gravitas.

UNIT 7 The natural world

2.02 (Page 82)

1. Taking care of pet rabbits is really easy. You just need to do a little planning. The first thing you need to do, before you even get the rabbits, is to buy a hutch, which is like a little house for the rabbit. Put the hutch in a place where it won't be exposed to cold winds or hot summer sun. Once you have your rabbits, basically you feed them twice a day. You have to make sure to get food that they like. It can be a little tricky, because they're sort of picky about what they eat. You have to clean out the hutch once a week or more, so you need fresh straw and hay.

   And you need to have them vaccinated against myxomatosis, a disease that affects rabbits. So, that's about it- they're a pretty easy pet to take care of.

2. It seems pretty straightforward, but actually there are a lot of things that can go wrong when you choose a dog. A lot of people, for example, just go for the cutest dog they can find, which is understandable, but really not the right way to choose a dog. The first thing you need to do is to ask yourself a few questions. Will you have enough time to walk the dog and give her attention? Can you afford a dog? People often forget that there are expenses involved in owning a dog—you have to pay a vet for vaccines and if the dog gets sick. Do you have enough space in the house? Once you've answered these questions, the next thing to think about is what type of dog would be best for you. If you buy a puppy, you need to consider how big and active it will be once it's grown up. Different breeds have different characteristics. If you have an active lifestyle it's OK to get a Chihuahua or a Doberman, but if you spend most of your time at home watching TV, get a less active dog, like a Saint Bernard. The most important thing is to do your research before you buy. Talk to other dog owners and vets, and read as much as you can.

2.03 (Page 82)

1
A: The first thing you need to do . . .

2
B: You just need to do a little planning.

3
A: You have to make sure to get food that they like.

4
B: You have to clean out the hutch once a week or more . . .

2.04 (Page 82)

1. A lot of people, for example, just go for the cutest dog they can find.
2. The first thing you need to do is to ask yourself a few questions.
3. The next thing to think about is what type of dog would be best for you.
4. If you spend most of your time at home watching TV, get a less active dog.

2.05 (Page 83)

A: The first thing I noticed when I entered the bureaucrat's office was that it was bright white, like a doctor's surgery or the cell of a madman. There were a few filing cabinets next to the desk and a huge photo of the king staring at us from the wall. The air was thick, and a fan droned weakly, whirring overhead as a gang of flies zig-zagged across the air.

The bureaucrat behind his desk looked up to greet me.

"How can I help you?" he said. I told him I needed a visa for my trip to the Danakil Depression, and he asked me if I'd ever been in a desert. "I've been in many," I replied. He shifted in his chair and said, "The Danakil Depression is the world's hottest place. It's not a tourist site. There's nothing there but hot air and salt." I told him I knew that, and that's why I wanted to go there. "Typical American," he said. "Obsessed by the weather."

He asked me what I'd do if I got lost, and I told him I wouldn't. "And what about the three s's?" he said. "What three s's?" "Snakes, spiders, and scorpions. What if you get bitten?" "I won't." He stared at me again, glanced at my passport, and with a resounding thump, stamped it. "One visa," he said. "This will get you into Danakil, but it won't get you out."

2.06 (Page 83)

A: Going to the Danakil Depression means walking into hell on Earth. The land is sunk more than 300 feet below sea level and the place is a furnace. The air shakes, warped by the sun. Even the wind brings no relief from the heat. Almost everything around you is dead: stumps of trees, cracked earth, the occasional white glow of animal bones.

Along the way we saw a group of bandits on camels, brandishing their weapons. They waved and went on riding. Salt statues loomed out of the spectacular landscape, nine feet high, vibrant colors and shapes from another world. An active volcano was hunched on the horizon, biding its time. We stopped to visit a ghost town, with its abandoned shacks stripped bare by the wind and the nomads and the scavenging animals. This was Danakil, where an American company had tried to set up a business in the sixties and had been defeated by the heat. The ruined buildings made of salt blocks were now crumbling away, and there were metal tracks in the ground where they had tried to build a railway but which now led nowhere.

For three days my shirt was drenched and my mouth parched. Even covered up against the sun, my skin baked and burned, and there seemed no escape from the cauldron of heat. They tell you to drink twelve liters of water a day, to remember to drink even when you're not thirsty, but it's never enough.

When we finally arrived at our destination I felt empty, as if everything had been a mistake. I didn't regret going to Danakil, but the land was so inhospitable that permanent settlement seemed impossible, and it felt wrong being there, as if we were trespassing on a place nature had intended only for itself.

2.07 (Page 86)

A: Sharon Edwards once spent a day in an airplane, looking for a cat. The plane flew around the world for three weeks before she found it. They sent the cat home first-class. Another time, she found two suitcases full of birds from Turkey. But her strangest experience was when she pulled a snake out of a man's clothing.

B: I'm an animal health inspector at Heathrow Airport. I look after the animals that pass through Heathrow. I check that they are healthy and legal, and sometimes I look after them when they are waiting for a connecting flight.

Here are the areas for dogs, cats, reptiles, birds and fish. Over there is the area for very big animals. The biggest we ever had here was a black rhino, absolutely enormous.

At the Animal Center here, we receive all types of animals—we've had chimpanzees, wild cats, poisonous spiders, and it's impossible for one person to know about all of these. It keeps you on your toes because you're always picking up new information about different breeds of animal. But there are twenty people working here and between us we share our expertise. There is also a library and the Internet if we have any problems. I recently had to feed a group of toucans, but luckily, Tesco's is open twenty-four hours, so I had to go out at 2 A.M. to buy bananas.

The most common animals are cats and dogs. They come in all the time. And also lots of little children arrive at Heathrow carrying their pet hamster in their pocket, so I have to look after it for a while. The children always look very contrite when they're caught, but we usually don't take any action. It's not what you'd really call smuggling!

I often work at night. It's very quiet between 1 and 4 A.M. because we don't have any night flights. We try and give the animals a night-time. We dim the lights, and it's peaceful. And you never know what the new day will bring.

2.08 **(Page 87)**

1. A monkey costs as little as that?
2. It's as big as an elephant.
3. We're as happy as can be.

2.09 **(Page 90)**

A: Well, it's a piece of land that's about 31 square miles, so there's really a lot you could do with it, but I don't really know much about managing land. Do you have any ideas about what we could do with it?

B: Well, when I see 31 square miles of land, I think money. I think . . .

A: Ha, that's typical!

B: Well, yeah. I think a hotel would be great there. There's enough room for it, and we could really sell the whole unspoiled-island aspect.

A: Yeah, but the problem with the hotel is that the land is so beautiful as is. It would be a shame to mess with that. Maybe it would be nicer to do something that's kind of more geared toward the environment. We could leave it wild and just let the animals roam free, or start an animal sanctuary.

B: What would we get out of that?

A: It's good for the environment, Greg. I mean, it's doing something good, and giving something back to the earth, and making sure that there's a little wildness left in this world.

B: Mm. OK. Maybe not a hotel then, but I think we could think of a commercial use that would fit in more with the environment. What about some kind of health resort, maybe?

A: Well that's a nice idea because there's so much land, and people could go walking in the hills, and we could do nature trails through the forest. We could even have a little organic garden or, provide food that's really fresh and healthy because the land's really good for growing vegetables and things like that. We could have an organic health spa. What do you think?

B: Hm . . . yeah, that's a nice idea.

UNIT 8 Problems and issues

2.10 **(Page 94)**

1. That's a good question. Hmmm. I think I'd like some kind of robot to clean the house and do the laundry. Either that or get a maid.
2. A time machine. Not so I could go back and see earlier civilizations and dinosaurs—I mean, who cares about dinosaurs?—but so I could go back this morning and get to work before that guy who took my parking space.
3. That's a difficult question. I'd have to think about it. Well, I wouldn't mind a weather machine, with me in control, of course. So when my friends go on vacation, I could make it rain every day and they'd stop telling me how beautiful the weather was.
4. That's tricky. How about a pill that you can substitute for food, so no one would need to starve? And so I wouldn't have to cook.
5. Let me see. You could have a pill that makes you extremely intelligent. You'd take it just before every test or whenever the computer breaks down.
6. Well, I'd like to invent a special device that could take you to other places but only in your mind. Like a hat or glasses that give you all the sensations of being there. Then I'd use the glasses to go straight to a beach in Hawaii and spend the week there.
7. I'd invent a clock that extends hours of the day when you need it. Like every morning when I'm lying in bed and don't want to get up.

2.11 **(Page 95)**

A: I was on a business trip in Rome a few years ago. I'd been having dinner with a client all evening, and afterwards I found myself desperately looking for a late-night Internet café to check my emails from the office. So there I was at midnight, wandering around one of the most beautiful cities in the world, and I was tearing my hair out trying to get access to a computer. Anyway, I went back to the hotel and thought, do I really have to live like this? Are those emails really so important? So I started to reassess my life.

The world is one stressed-out place. When I go to cities now, I see everybody rushing around with their smart phones and laptops, and everyone's scared they're going to miss something. Y'know, no one ever looks back on their life and says, "I wish I'd spent more time working in the office."

After leaving my job, I moved to the beach. I sell surfing gear now. It doesn't make much money, but then money isn't the be-all and end-all. I'm happier than ever before, I think because living by the ocean gives you a certain perspective on life. The waves will be rolling in every morning long after we're gone. And it makes you realize all that hurrying isn't going to make any difference.

B: I've been working at an investment company for about four years. It's a very competitive business, of course, and you have to know about every fluctuation in the market right as it's happening. So I live a very fast-paced, high-pressure lifestyle. Actually, my friends tell me I suffer from a disease called "running out of time syndrome."

A lot of my work is done on the move, so I carry my office around with me: laptop, smart phone, electronic notepad. I suppose you could call these my weapons of war! They're a security blanket really.

I don't live a particularly healthy lifestyle: I grab a sandwich when I can, and drink far too much coffee. But it's not going to be like this forever. Most people in my profession burn out after three and a half years. In fact, the statistics are getting worse—I think it's under three years now. So by the time I'm forty, forty-five, I'll be slowing down a bit. But I don't think I'll ever live on a farm in the middle of nowhere growing vegetables. I'd hate that. I enjoy the buzz too much.

2.12 **(Page 99)**

Conversation 1

A: This stupid thing keeps getting jammed.

B: What, again?

A: I can't get it to make any copies.

B: It happened to me yesterday. Give it a good kick. Is that better?

A: Well, I feel better, yeah, but it's still not working.

Conversation 2

C: See? I always get the same message.

D: You have performed an illegal operation. That sounds bad.

C: See? I don't know how to make it shut down normally.

D: Have you tried dropping it on the floor?

C: What?

D: Or shouting at it? That works sometimes.

C: You're not funny.

Conversation 3

E: I'm having a problem turning it on.

F: Oh really?

E: This thing seems to be stuck. It won't turn.

F: Oh.

E: Which means I can't get any air in here. And it's so hot.

F: The middle of summer is a bad time for it to break. You can always open the windows.

E: Oh! Yeah, thanks.

UNIT 9 People with vision

2.13 **(Page 106)**

A: What can you tell us about what happens when geniuses relax?

B: Without a doubt, we can be sure that great scientists don't always make their discoveries in the lab. Archimedes's famous Eureka moment came while he was having a bath. Physicist Richard Feynman saw a plate flying through the air in a college cafeteria, and was inspired to calculate electron orbits. He later won the Nobel Prize. And Alexander Fleming was making mold for his hobby, microbe painting, when he accidentally came across *Penicillium notatum*, later known as penicillin.

A: So what does this tell us?

B: Well, a recent study by Robert Root-Bernstein compared the hobbies of 134 Nobel prize winning chemists to those of other scientists. He found that the Nobel prize winners were accomplished outside the lab as well. Over half were artistic, and almost all had a long-lasting hobby. Twenty-five percent of the Nobel prize winners played a musical instrument, and eighteen percent drew or painted regularly. Of the non-Nobel winners, under one percent had a hobby.

A: Fascinating. So should we conclude that only a creative person can be a genius?

B: Well, I think that's debatable. Perhaps it's true up to a point, but I don't think it's as clear-cut as that. What we do know is that to a certain extent, creative thinking can help people to solve problems, even scientific ones. That if you are thinking about a problem all the time, often the answer eludes you. But it may come in an inspiration when you are least expecting it—perhaps when you're asleep, or thinking about other things, doing a hobby, for example. It's not 100 percent certain, but it seems that the mind has the ability to make connections from one part of your life to another, so that actually stepping back from a problem can often provide the answer. And people who are good at making these connections, people who pursue creative hobbies and interests, often excel in their particular fields.

2.14 (Page 107)

Every year, at the National Portrait Gallery in London, there is a competition for the best portrait. The winner is decided democratically: everyone who visits the exhibition can vote for their favorite portrait. Listen to some visitors to the exhibit.

Conversation 1

A: What do you think of this one?
B: Um . . . it's OK. To be honest, it's not really my taste. It sort of looks like a photo to me.
C: Yeah, you have to get up really close to it to see that it's a painting.
A: What do you think of it?
C: I really like it, actually.
A: Me too.
C: I like the colors, and the expression on her face is kind of intense.
A: It's a little bit enigmatic, isn't it? You don't really know what she's thinking. And the details are great, too—You can almost see the pores of her skin.
B: Well, as I was saying, it really does look like a photo—the detail is amazing. But to tell you the truth, I still wouldn't want it hanging on my bedroom wall.

Conversation 2

A: I love this one.
C: He has such an interesting face, doesn't he? He looks like a hippie poet from the Seventies.
A: That's some beard.
B: I like the blanket over his shoulders.
C: And the medallion.
A: Oh yeah, I didn't notice that.
C: As a matter of fact, I like this one better than the other one. At any rate, I think it's more interesting.
A: How about this one for your bedroom wall?
B: Nope. 'Fraid not.

Conversation 3

B: I think this one's great.
C: It's kind of menacing isn't it?
B: For me, what's interesting is that they are in a group, almost like a gang. And they're all dressed pretty much the same.
C: The jeans and white T-shirt.
B: Exactly, except for the guy sitting in the middle. He's the only one sitting and looking directly at us, sort of challenging us, so maybe he's the boss.
A: Well, what I noticed is that, as you said, they're in a group, but somehow they look isolated. They're all facing in different directions, and they don't seem to relate to each other at all.
C: And I wonder why it's called La Familia. They obviously aren't a family in any traditional sense. At any rate, they don't look like a family, so it's kind of intriguing. I think this one should win, actually.
A: Me too.

2.15 (Page 107)

C: So which one won in the end?
A: Which do you think?
C: Well, as I said before, my favorite is La Familia, but . . .
A: That one didn't win.
C: Oh really?
A: The winner was Giulietta Coates, the one that looks like a photo.
C: Well, I think it's really good too, but it isn't my favorite.

2.16 (Page 114)

A: Clarence Birdseye was a taxidermist from New York. On a visit to the Arctic he saw how the native people preserved their food by putting it in barrels of sea water, which froze quickly. This way, the food maintained its freshness for later. So in 1923 he bought a seven-dollar electric fan, some ice, and some buckets of salt water and experimented by putting food in them. Birdseye's experiments worked, and he went on to become the pioneer of frozen foods in the western world. In 1929 he sold the patent for 22 million dollars and in 1930 frozen food went on sale for the first time in the United States.
B: As a young man, Chester Carlson's job involved making multiple copies of patent documents by hand. Writing everything down was difficult for Carlson because he was short-sighted and had arthritis, so in 1938 he invented a machine to make copies. He tried to get funding for his idea from all sorts of well-known companies, including IBM and General Electric, but they turned him down. Eventually the company that became Xerox bought his idea, and the first photocopier was manufactured in 1959. Now there's hardly an office in the world that doesn't contain his invention.

UNIT 10 Expressing feelings

2.17 (Page 116)

A: Today we have psychologist Walter Bright with us to talk about optimism and pessimism. Welcome, Dr. Bright.
B: Thank you, Kathryn. It's a pleasure to be here.
A: So, Dr. Bright—Optimism vs. pessimism. My mom is the queen optimist. She waltzes her way through life blissfully happy. She sees a positive side to everything. My dad is the polar opposite—he can't see the positive in anything. When I had a car accident as a teen and crashed the family car, Mom focused on the fact that I was OK. Dad, on the other hand, almost had a nervous breakdown because the car was totaled. He reprimanded me for being a careless driver and didn't let me behind the wheel for six months. (He still won't let me forget that incident, either.) (chuckle)
B: Well, what a perfect example of seeing the glass half full or half empty! We are all born with a predisposition to a more positive or negative way of thinking. Optimists believe that they influence positive events in their lives, but that negative events just happen.
A: So in my mom's eyes, the accident wasn't my fault.
B: Exactly. There must have been some other reason for the accident. Whereas pessimists believe that they are responsible for the negative events that happen to them. So your dad clearly saw you as being responsible for the car accident. And being a pessimist, he most likely saw more such failures for you ahead.
A: That about sums up my dad . . .
B: Now, in turn, if something good happens, an optimist believes that she is directly responsible. So, let's use your mom as an example. What was her reaction when you got your first job?
A: She was beyond thrilled, of course.
B: And in her optimistic thinking, it was proof that more good things will happen to you. Now, what was your dad's reaction when you got that job?
A: Well, he was shocked. I mean, he was happy, I guess. But clearly he thought it was a total fluke that someone would hire me.
B: Classic! When something good happens, pessimists see it as chance and as something that probably won't happen again.
A: Wow, seems like pessimists would be more prone to depression.
B: Well, depression is complex, with a variety of different causes—mental, physical, social. But, yes, a person with a negative outlook is more likely to be depressed than an optimistic person.
A: So what is the verdict? Clearly the optimists out there will be OK. Are all of us pessimists doomed?
B: Ha ha. No, you're not doomed. We're not doomed. I'm a pessimist by nature, too! While we tend to be predisposed to think negatively, we can learn positive patterns of thinking.
A: I don't know. As much as my mom tried to instill her optimism in me when I was growing up, her Mary Sunshine disposition was lost on me. I'm sure I'm even further gone now in adulthood.
B: Not necessarily. With cognitive restructuring, you can train yourself to become more optimistic. You just need to be aware of your negative thoughts and replace them with positive thinking. I can't exactly call myself a converted optimist, but I have significantly improved my pessimistic ways, thanks to cognitive restructuring.
A: So, what would I do to think more positively?
B: You need to define positive things that happen in your life as being caused by you and as proof that more good things are bound to happen to you.
A: So, getting a talented psychologist to do this interview was my doing, and I should look forward to landing more interesting people to interview.

B: That's right, exactly! And negative events that occur, you might think about whether they are due to something you did, or whether they are just isolated occurrences that will not have an effect on the future. You must guard against assuming that you are automatically responsible for everything bad that happens.

A: So, my poor tennis game this past week—I shouldn't be too bummed about that?

B: Definitely not! Think of extenuating circumstances that might have contributed to the game. Were you worried about something? Maybe sleep deprived? Or maybe you just had an off day. Whatever it was, the temporary failure wasn't a reflection of personal weakness! Also, part of cognitive restructuring is the idea that you have endless opportunities to improve in the future.

A: Well, if you put it that way, then I'm inspired. Looking forward to my next potential success! (cynical)

B: That's the idea. And no need to be cynical! Remember, if you can embrace optimism at least on some level, you will reap all sorts of benefits: physical health, greater achievement, emotional health, increased longevity, less stress, and on and on . . .

A: True! Well, thank you for being our guest, Dr. Bright. This was truly informational! And can I ask you—your name, by the way—did you change it as part of your cognitive restructuring?

B: Ha, ha. No. But let's say it's been an inspiration trying to live up to my name!

2.18 (Page 119)

1. I've often wondered what it was like to have been in the first airplane to take off and really fly, not just like the Wright Brothers' first plane going for a ten or thirty second hop, but really climbing into the air. It couldn't have been easy, because those aircraft were not very sophisticated. They must have been difficult to fly—physically and even mentally—and they would've had to do lots of calculations that no one else had done before. But of course it would have been so exhilarating as they got higher and higher. And then coming in for the landing. How would that have been? It must have been something close to a controlled crash. Even so, what a thrill.

2. It must have been amazing to be the first modern person to see Machu Picchu, after it had been covered by jungle for so long. I think it must have been pretty hard to get there, because nowadays they've built a train, and it's easier to get to. But, the first modern people that went there had to climb right up the side of the huge mountain without knowing that there was anything there at the top, so they must have been really driven. But, although they might have felt the same atmosphere when they arrived, it couldn't have been quite as spectacular as it is today because the ruins now are there for you to see as soon as you arrive. It must have had more of a mysterious air when they discovered it covered in vegetation and all hidden, without really knowing what it was.

3. I think Yuri Gagarin must have had mixed emotions about being the first person in space. On the one hand, there's that sort of thrill and excitement of space travel, and the absolute awe of what he was experiencing, being the first person to see Earth from space, having never even had any concept of what it might look like. The vastness of space must have been amazing, too. But on the other hand, he was up there on his own, basically in a tin can—anything could have happened up there. He probably didn't know if he would get back home or not. He must have felt alone and I would think pretty scared as well.

2.19 (Page 122)

1. During my childhood my parents moved a lot, so I was always changing schools. In fact, in about six years I think we moved three times. It was hard, because just when I'd made new friends and gotten used to the teachers and the school, I had to do it all again. I got pretty lonely, and I found it difficult to relate to other children, especially because they all knew the area, they already had their small groups of friends, and I was slightly out of it. But it also made me very outgoing, because if I wasn't going to be outgoing and energetic, and entertaining, I was never going to make friends. So, I suppose that's one good thing that came from all those moves—I have lots of friends in many places.

2. I think one of my worst memories from childhood is probably a sports-related memory. I'm not very athletic, you see. I grew up in a pretty big city, and our gym teacher used to make us go cross-country running every week, so we'd be out there, in the rain, and the wind, in the middle of the city, with the traffic roaring by, running around in our gym clothes—I hated it. I used to dread Mondays, because that's when we had gym class. I'm still the same. I still hate sports, and running is one of the sports I hate the most. I know some people love it, but I just can't seem to enjoy it no matter what. So I would say running in gym class is one of the worst memories from my childhood.

3. When I was a child we used to go to Majorca nearly every year. It was a family vacation—my grandparents came, too. I think the last time I was there I was about seven. Maybe eight. The thing I remember most vividly is arriving in Majorca, and this wall of heat that would hit us when we got off the plane. The air smelled so different from home. It was a wonderful smell. And I remember the things that children remember about vacations—I remember the pool, and how blue it was—we used to swim every day. And the breakfasts that went on forever—the routine was completely different from what we did at home. We met people there from all over the world. We made friends with a Norwegian family one year and kept in touch with them for many years. I haven't been back since then, because I don't really want to spoil my memories of it. I think the magic might be lost if I were to see it now as an adult.

4. During the summer, I lived in the woods. Well, actually, our property was next to a beautiful forest. I used to climb over the fence, and my friends and I used to play in the woods all day. We used to climb trees, run in and out of bushes, and basically run around free all summer. It was such a great feeling of freedom—something every kid should have.

2.20 (Page 126)

1. Wow. I went to the most amazing restaurant last night. You would not believe it. I'd never been anywhere like that before. The name of the restaurant was Aria. It was on one of those cute little streets down by the river—the owners had renovated one of those adorable old buildings. It's such a wonderful blend of old and modern—the old architecture, with very modern décor in the dining rooms. The service was incredible—the servers were all really polite and charming, but not too obtrusive. The food was what I would call modern French, and it was out of this world. We had what they call a "tasting menu," which consisted of lots of small courses. It was pretty expensive but sooo delicious that it was worth it.

2. I cannot stand public transportation in this country. I mean, despite the fact that it's expensive and unreliable, it's just so unnecessarily complicated. Just look at trains, for example. There must be about twenty different ticket types. And it all depends on when you're traveling, what time of day, how far in advance you buy your ticket, etc. It's just ridiculous. For example, you could be sitting on a train, and the person sitting next to you could've paid twice as much for their ticket just because they happened to buy it on a different day. I don't understand why we don't have a system like in other countries, where you just pay one price for each distance, and maybe a little more for an express train. As it stands now, it's just too complicated.

3. I really hate smoking, and I think it should be banned altogether. It's really unfair for those of us who don't smoke—you go to a restaurant or café, and you have to breathe in other people's smoke. Then you smell like smoke for the rest of the day. I mean, smoking is obviously not good for the smoker of course, but it's not good for the non-smokers, either. If you don't smoke, it's really disgusting to have to breathe in second-hand smoke. And I don't buy it when smokers say, "Well, we'll just sit in a part of the restaurant where it doesn't affect you, or we'll go outside." You know what, it does affect us, because even if you're outside, and you're walking behind somebody who is smoking, you're breathing in their smoke. And don't get me started on people who smoke around children. I think it should just be banned, because it's one of the few bad habits that really does affect everybody else.

ENGLISH in Common 6B

Workbook

Antonia Clare and JJ Wilson

Series Consultants
María Victoria Saumell and Sarah Louisa Birchley

ALWAYS LEARNING PEARSON

UNIT 6
Understanding power

LESSON 1
Reading

1a Read the news story and answer the questions on a separate sheet of paper.

1. What is the purpose of the international vote?
2. What happened to the original seven wonders?

New wonders of the world

They have sheltered kings, protected nations from invaders, inspired the world's greatest artists, and spawned a million postcards. Now the world's most glorified buildings are to be officially recognized, not by the United Nations, or by architects, but by the common man and woman, or at least those with Internet access.

Millions of people are taking part in an international vote to pick seven new wonders of the world. The contenders include: the Statue of Liberty; Petra, in Jordan; the Colosseum; the Acropolis; and the statue of Christ the Redeemer, in Rio de Janeiro. The campaign, via the modern wonder of the Internet, was launched by adventurer, filmmaker, and entrepreneur Bernard Weber, who says he wants to create a definitive list, chosen in a democratic fashion.

After an initial weeding-out process, 21 wonders remain, the final seven of which will be determined by the number of votes cast in their favor on www.new7wonders.com. The winning sites will be filmed by Mr. Weber. However, not everyone is happy with the short list. The absence of technology disappointed Stuart Leslie, a professor at Johns Hopkins University. He claims that the Internet should be on the list, simply because it allows us to access all the other wonders. Mr. Leslie's list would also include inventions such as the hydrogen bomb and nylon.

Of the old seven wonders, only one still exists: the Great Pyramid of Giza. The others have been destroyed over the years by a combination of earthquakes, fire, and greed, as invaders ransacked palaces and temples. Though Weber admits he has no idea how long the new seven wonders will last, he's having a lot of fun naming them.

b Read the story again and take notes under the headings.

The voting process ______________________

____

Bernard Weber ______________________

____

Criticisms of the new list ______________________

____

c Circle the best definition. Use the news story to help you.

1. spawn (*v.*)
   - **a.** take photos using advanced technology
   - **b.** inspire others to copy something, or produce or generate something
2. contender (*n.*)
   - **a.** a type of building found in ancient cities
   - **b.** person or thing taking part in a competition
3. definitive (*adj.*)
   - **a.** final/complete/able to serve as a perfect example
   - **b.** long-lasting
4. weed out (*v.*)
   - **a.** remove the worst or weakest from a list or group
   - **b.** put forward an argument for the one you think is the best
5. short list (*n.*)
   - **a.** winner, following a long discussion
   - **b.** group of the best candidates for final consideration (in a competition)
6. ransack (*v.*)
   - **a.** change the structure of a building by adding parts
   - **b.** search violently in order to steal something

Grammar

2 Choose a, an, the, or no article (–).

Easter Island

Easter Island is a/an/the/– (1.) remote place 2,200 miles off a/an/the/– (2.) coast of Chile. It has barely 4,000 inhabitants, one airport, and some simple accommodations for tourists. It used to be full of a/an/the/– (3.) lush trees, but they died centuries ago. Yet, Easter Island is world famous. There are few more powerful and mysterious sights than a/an/the/– (4.) island's magnificent statues, called moai, rising up out of the barren landscape thirteen feet high and weighing fourteen tons.

These huge stone heads were carved from a/an/the/– (5.) volcanic rock between four and nine hundred years ago. With their elongated faces and deep-set eyes, they are a/an/the/– (6.) incredibly haunting sight, and there are 887 of them. But what was their purpose?

A/An/The/– (7.) archeologists suggest that a/an/the/– (8.) statues were symbols of religious and political power, or perhaps depictions of the spirits of early ancestors. There are other mysteries surrounding a/an/the/– (9.) moai. They were not built where they are found, so how were they transported? What's more, the majority of the moai have been knocked down and now lie on their faces or in a/an/the/– (10.) pieces. Why? We will probably never know.

3 Add or cross out one word to complete each sentence. One sentence is correct.

1. The Taj Mahal is probably most famous building in India.
2. The Ice Hotel, in Quebec, is made up entirely from ice.
3. Maya Ying Lin designed a famous wall in Washington, D.C. as memorial for the soldiers who died in Vietnam.
4. The Arc de Triomphe, in Paris, was built honor of Napoleon's military conquests.
5. Covering an area of a million square feet, Paris's Pompidou Center is one of Europe's greatest cultural centers.
6. The Great Wall of China is about 4,000 miles long and eight yards up high.
7. The Mayan pyramids may have been used for to house the bodies of kings.
8. Turkey's greatest church, the Hagia Sophia, is said to have built in just five years.

Writing

4 Read the notes about two pieces of architecture that didn't go according to plan. Choose one and write a short essay about it. Use phrases from page 70 of the Student Book to help you.

Leaning Tower of Pisa
- a bell tower, next to Pisa Cathedral, Pisa, Italy
- started 1173, completed 1372 (wars prevented completion)
- architect: Pisano and di Simone + others??
- problem: tower began to sink during construction, as soil settled
- 1272: engineers built upper floors with one side taller than the other to compensate for building's tilt
- 1990–2001: closed for repairs and reconstruction. Now stable for next 300 years.

Empire State Building
- skyscraper, New York City, USA
- started 1930, opened May 1, 1931
- architect: William F. Lamb
- problem: strong winds made building unstable
- builders designed special framework
- building became so solid that it was easily repaired when a plane crashed into it in 1945!

LESSON 2

Reading

1a Read the article quickly and choose the best sub-heading.

1. How technology is changing the way our students learn
2. Email etiquette in college
3. How professors and students keep in touch

Student power

(1) One student skipped class and then sent the professor an email message asking for copies of the teaching notes. Another didn't like her grade and sent a petulant message to the professor. Another explained that she was late for a Monday class because she was recovering from a party. One professor received a message from a student, saying "I'm not sure how to shop for school supplies. Should I buy a binder or a subject notebook? Would you let me know your recommendations?" At colleges and universities, email has made professors more approachable, but many say it has made them too accessible. They say that students seem to view them as available around the clock, sending a steady stream of email messages—from ten a week to ten after every class—that are too informal or simply inappropriate. Michael J. Kessler, a lecturer at Georgetown University, says, "The tone that they take in an email is pretty astounding, 'I need to know this and you need to tell me right now.' It's a fine balance to accommodate what they need and at the same time maintain a level of legitimacy as an instructor. We are authorized to make demands on them, and not the other way around."

(2) Professor Patricia Ewick, of Clark University, Massachusetts, said ten students emailed her drafts of their papers days before they were due, seeking comments. Ewick says, "It's all different levels of presumption. One is that I'll be able to drop everything and read 250 pages two days before I'm going to get fifty of these." Robert B. Ahdieh, associate professor of law, said he had received emails with messages such as "you're covering the material too fast" or "I don't think we're using the reading as much as we could in class" or "I think it would be helpful if you would summarize what we've covered at the end of class in case we missed anything." While once professors expected deference, their expertise seems to have become just another service that students, as consumers, are buying. So, students may have no fear of giving offense or imposing on the professor's time. Many professors say they are uncertain how to react to the emails. For example, the professor who was asked about buying the notebook said she debated whether to tell the student that this was not a query that should be directed to her, but worried that "such a message could be pretty scary" and decided not to respond at all.

(3) Most professors, however, emphasized that instant feedback could be invaluable. One professor said that questions about a lecture or discussion indicated "a blind spot," that the student obviously didn't understand something. Others have probably hit on the best solution by making rules for email: telling students how quickly the professor would respond, how messages should be drafted, and what type of messages they would answer. Meg Worley, an assistant professor of English, tells students that they must say thank you after receiving a professor's response to an email. "The less powerful person always has to write back," she said.

b Complete the notes using information from the article.

- In higher education, professors are now more ____________ (1.) than they used to be because of ____________ (2.).
- The problem: students either write too ____________ (3.) emails or write emails that are ____________ (4.) (maybe too informal or thoughtless).
- Kessler says he doesn't like the ____________ (5.) of the emails he receives.
- Ewick thinks that students these days ____________ (6.) too much and seem to think that their teachers have a lot of free ____________ (7.).
- Ahdieh received criticisms of his ____________ (8.) by email.
- A lot of professors aren't ____________ (9.) how to respond to these emails.
- Some professors have solved the problem by making ____________ (10.) about email use.

c Check the sentences that are true, according to the article.

____ **1.** The professors said that students rarely missed lessons without good reasons. (paragraph 1)

____ **2.** Some students write angry emails and behave like children. (paragraph 1)

____ **3.** As a professor, you have to maintain your credibility in front of students. (paragraph 1)

____ **4.** One professor asked students to email the first version of their compositions. (paragraph 2)

____ **5.** Students' emails show that the traditional humility toward professors isn't as common as it used to be. (paragraph 2)

____ **6.** Many professors said that receiving criticisms by email was extremely useful to them. (paragraph 3)

____ **7.** Emails about lectures sometimes showed there was an area that the student didn't grasp very well. (paragraph 3)

____ **8.** Some professors found a perfect answer to the problem by banning email correspondence. (paragraph 3)

d Find words or expressions in the article that have the same meaning as the underlined words or expressions in Exercise 1c.

Grammar

2 Six of these sentences contain mistakes. Check the correct sentences and correct the mistakes in the others.

____ **1.** I'll vote for who has the best economic plan.

____ **2.** Roberto is your driver. Where you want to go, he will take you.

____ **3.** Whatever we want to do, we have to get permission from the boss.

____ **4.** How you look at it, whether you are an employee or a customer, it's a stupid rule.

____ **5.** Whenever the teacher comes into the room, the students stand up.

____ **6.** What you said, I didn't hear you because of the music.

____ **7.** I'll talk to whoever I can in order to get you an interview.

____ **8.** Who you spoke to, it wasn't the boss, but an impersonator!

____ **9.** Help me however you can.

____ **10.** Wherever I go, that beautiful woman seems to follow.

____ **11.** How you choose to join, whether online or in person, it is a great deal.

3 Circle the correct choices to complete the paragraph.

Parent Power

Desperate parents in Gigo, New Zealand, decided to write a manifesto for the children in the town, following a rise in bad behavior. "I'm not sure why/however (**1.**) it got so bad, but whatever/whenever (**2.**) one of us tried to discipline our kids, they would just swear at us," says Joe Malonga. "Whatever/However (**3.**) we tried to do, it failed. We tried bribing them, punishing them, and eventually begging them. Nothing worked." So, whenever/when (**4.**) Malonga suggested drawing up a list of rules, other parents agreed immediately. "Who/Whoever (**5.**) thought of a rule had to be backed by 70% of the parents. Then, we persuaded the kids to sign the document, and posted hundreds of copies around town." Where/Wherever (**6.**) you look—in stores, schools, bus stops—you can see Gigo's Twelve Golden Rules. "So far it's worked like a charm," says Malonga.

Vocabulary

4 Circle the correct word or words to complete each sentence.

1. This is our new product. We're hoping it will catch in Asia especially.
a. up **b.** off **c.** on

2. Revolutions tend to come because of desperation on a huge scale.
a. through **b.** on **c.** about

3. According to fashion guru Leila Winston, lacy stockings are this winter, and every woman should have a pair.
a. off **b.** in **c.** up

4. It can be difficult to keep the news on the island, because the mail only comes once a month, and there's no Internet.
a. up with **b.** up to **c.** on with

5. The company decided to home new technology, focusing its attention on digital software.
a. in to **b.** in on **c.** up to

6. While hats were trendy last summer, they seem to be this year.
a. on **b.** off **c.** out

Communication

1 Read the conversation on the right. Then mark the statements true (*T*) or false (*F*).

____ 1. Pete thinks that people sometimes confuse fame and charisma.

____ 2. Joan doesn't like movie stars much.

____ 3. Joan thinks athletes are often charismatic.

____ 4. Joan believes that most politicians have a little bit of charisma.

____ 5. Ann is surprised by Joan's opinions.

Grammar

2 Cross out the choice that is NOT possible.

1. The waiter didn't bring the food until midnight, *by which time/at which point/despite* Sarah was starving.
2. *No sooner had I arrived than/I'd hardly arrived when/On arriving*, Don left.
3. *Although/When/While* we like pasta, we don't want to eat it every day.
4. He finished the race *despite/even though/although* he felt sick.
5. We can't understand your theory, *much as/in spite/hard as* we try.
6. *On falling asleep/She hardly falls asleep/No sooner does she fall asleep than* she starts snoring.
7. No one goes to bed before 2 A.M. *during the festival/while the festival is going on/as long as the festival is*.
8. *Although/Despite/In spite of* your behavior, everyone had a good time yesterday.

Charisma . . . same as fame?

Pete: I'm never quite sure if people are really charismatic or if it's just something having to do with fame. Being famous kind of makes you automatically charismatic.

Ann: Like when a movie star walks into a restaurant, you mean, and everyone turns and stares and says: "Oh, what charisma," but actually it's just that the person's famous.

Pete: Exactly.

Joan: I think most famous people actually have no charisma whatsoever. Most movie stars are short, ugly, boring, and self-obsessed, which is just another way of being boring, of course.

Pete: Do you really think so?

Joan: Oh yeah, half of them are tiny. And they have bad skin.

Ann: Well, athletes are usually pretty impressive, physically.

Joan: True, but they don't have anything to say. They spend their whole lives in the gym, so as soon as they open their mouths, out comes a stream of nonsense.

Pete: But don't you think some of them are charismatic? Muhammad Ali or Pelé, people like that.

Joan: No.

Ann: What do you mean "no"?!

Joan: Well, if it wasn't for his achievements in a boxing ring, Ali would just be a loudmouth. I don't think that's charismatic at all. Same with all performing artists. They are good at one thing and then everyone assumes that they have some magical, mystical power like charisma. I don't buy it.

Pete: OK.

Ann: OK, well what about politicians? They must have some charisma in order for people to follow them.

Joan: Are you kidding? I'd say about .01% of politicians are charismatic. Most of them have lots of money behind them and a big political party that tells them what to say and wear and do, and how many babies to kiss.

Ann: I never knew you were so cynical, Joan.

3 Circle the best words or phrases below to complete the paragraphs.

Smart cop

An instructor had been explaining leadership to a group of police recruits from 8:00 to 1:00, ____ (**1.**) they were tired and hungry. Finally, the instructor gave one man secret instructions that he had to "get everyone out of here without causing panic." The recruit didn't know what to do. The instructor called a second man to the front. ____ (**2.**) the note, the recruit said, "The instructor wants us to go outside. Go!" No one moved. A third man looked at the instructions, smiled and said, "Break for lunch!" ____ (**3.**) the room emptied in seconds.

Mozart's Memory

When Mozart was a boy, his father took him to Rome. ____ (**4.**) their trip, they attended a service at St. Peter's Cathedral. Part of the music used in the service was a highly guarded secret, never shared with outsiders. As they listened, Mozart's father noticed his son's fascination with the music. That night, they ____ (**5.**) home when Mozart sat down and played the entire musical score, note for note. ____ (**6.**) the Vatican's best efforts, the secret was no match for Mozart's incredible memory!

A new page

Incredibly ____ (**9.**), Google is no traditional workplace, and co-founder Larry Page is said to be a charismatic, as well as unorthodox, boss. Page once made the staff attend a meeting wearing pink wigs, and he even tried to ban phones from a Google building. ____ (**10.**), he was told that the law required a phone in the elevators.

Thirsty soldiers

____ (**7.**) marching across the desert with his thirsty army, Alexander the Great was offered a helmet of water by one of his soldiers. Alexander said, "Is there enough for 10,000 men?" The soldier had no answer, and ____ (**8.**) Alexander was dying of thirst himself, he poured the water onto the ground.

	a.	b.	c.
1.	by this time	at this time	by which time
2.	By reading	On reading	To read
3.	at which point	at this point	to the point that
4.	While	In the middle	During
5.	had hardly returned	was already return	had sooner returned
6.	Although	In spite	Despite
7.	During	While	On
8.	in spite of	much as	even though
9.	successful as is	successful as it is	as it is successful
10.	However	He'd hardly started	Even though

Vocabulary

4 Complete the puzzle and find the key word. Look on page 76 of the Student Book if necessary.

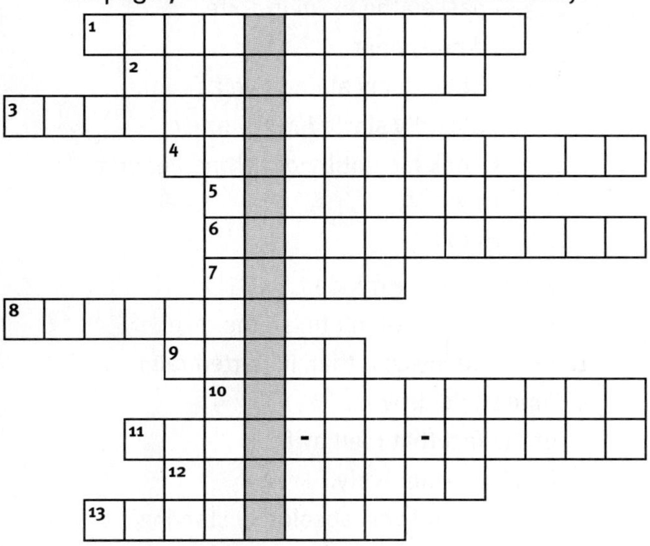

1. has a magnetic character that makes people want to follow (*adj.*)
2. is well-respected because he or she is calm and serious (*adj.*)
3. believes people should live according to high moral standards and principles (*adj.*)
4. is easy to talk to and friendly (*adj.*)
5. never stops working because he or she has lots of energy (*adj.*)
6. can be trusted completely (*adj.*)
7. is unable to make a decision, often ____s (*v.*)
8. accepts money illegally for favors (*adj.*)
9. is energetic and determined, has ____ (*n.*)
10. is not recognizable or interesting (*adj.*)
11. is practical and direct in a sensible, honest way (*adj.*)
12. is respected for his or her intellectual seriousness, has ____ (*n.*)
13. is determined and won't change his or her mind (*adj.*)

Key word ____________

UNIT 6 Review

1 Each of these sentences has one or two mistakes. Find the mistakes and correct them.

1. The dogs are generally considered the best pets for the elderly.
2. We thought we heard burglar, but later we realized that a noise was actually the pipes.
3. He climbed the Mt. Kilimanjaro when he was still the teenager.
4. As a child, she learned to play a piano and later went on to become the composer.
5. I'll see you at a supermarket at 8:00. Don't be late!
6. It's hard for the people like me to diet, because we love the chocolate.
7. Canada has introduced law to help newly-arrived immigrants find work.
8. I dreamed that I crossed Pacific Ocean in an old wooden boat!
9. Italian national anthem is one of my favorites.
10. We spoke to CEO of the company last night.

2 Circle the correct sentence(s) in each pair. Both may be correct.

1. **a.** Who you are, come out now with your hands up!
   b. Whoever you are, come out now with your hands up!
2. **a.** However hard I tried, it was never good enough for my father.
   b. How hard I tried, it was never good enough for my father.
3. **a.** You'll need to explain whatever you did, in very clear English.
   b. You'll need to explain what you did, in very clear English.
4. **a.** When you want to come over, just give me a call.
   b. Whenever you want to come over, just give me a call.
5. **a.** It seems that whichever option we choose, it's going to be costly.
   b. It seems that which option we choose, it's going to be costly.
6. **a.** This pocket knife will be useful where you're going.
   b. This pocket knife will be useful wherever you're going.

3 Circle the correct word or expression.

A friend forever

Desperate, Nick Bines broke into the home of a wealthy businessman, intending to steal jewelry and other valuables. He had *hardly/sooner* (1.) begun the burglary when he looked at the sideboard and, to his surprise, saw himself in a framed photo. The photo showed a group of teenagers on a fishing trip. Bines went to the living room and looked at other photos on display, *although/at which point* (2.) he realized that he was robbing the home of his best friend from school, Michael Pasha, whom he hadn't seen for ten years. *Much/Hard* (3.) as he needed the money, Bines decided to put everything back in its place. He had begun to climb out of the window *whenever/when* (4.) he caught his leg on the frame, fell, and broke his ankle. He *had no sooner/by this time* (5.) started crawling away along the side of the street than Michael Pasha's car pulled up. *Although/On* (6.) seeing his old friend in this state, Pasha took Bines inside. *In spite of the fact/While* (7.) they were talking, it soon became obvious what had happened. *In spite/Despite* (8.) of this, instead of reporting his old friend to the police, Pasha took Bines to the hospital, and a month later, gave him a job.

4 Match the beginning of each sentence to its end.

____ 1. I'd walked for six hours, at
____ 2. Much as I love him,
____ 3. I passed the exam in spite
____ 4. I'd no sooner
____ 5. Although my alarm didn't go off,
____ 6. I'd hardly started my journey
____ 7. It took me until 2:00 to find her number, by which
____ 8. Hard as I

a. when my tire exploded.
b. tried, I just couldn't finish the race.
c. taken off my coat than it started raining.
d. time she'd arrived.
e. of the fact that I felt awful.
f. I still woke up early.
g. which point I was absolutely starving.
h. I really don't want to get married now.

5 Rewrite the sentences using the correct form of the word in parentheses.

1. You must stay up-to-date with developments in your field. (keep)
You must ______________________________
______________________________.
2. Those pants are trendy these days. (in)
Those pants ______________________________.
3. The idea originated because of something I read. (come)
The idea ______________________________
______________________________.
4. The company is targeting the children's market. (home)
The company is ______________________________
______________________________.
5. That fashion will grow popular very quickly. (catch)
That fashion will ______________________________
______________________________.
6. Style gurus tell us that long hair is no longer in style. (out)
Style gurus tell us that long hair ______________.

6 Complete the news headlines with words from the box.

consumer	brain	in positions	wind
comes to	world	special powers	

1. Scientists hail ____________ power as answer to energy crisis.
2. Ten-year-old genius uses ____________ power to solve ancient puzzle!
3. China is fast emerging as the new ____________ power.
4. Supermarket boss says ____________ power is forcing food companies to "go organic" as customers walk away.
5. Report says corruption is on the rise among people ____________ of power.
6. Political party ____________ power after twenty years in the wilderness.
7. Government grants ____________ to anti-terrorist squad.

7 Circle the best words or phrases below to complete the paragraph.

Chad Thomson is ____ **(1.)** speaker—he had the audience in the palm of his hand at the Clovell Center on Tuesday. His theme was that business leaders no longer have to be incredibly ____ **(2.)**; the era of the superhero CEO is over. Leaders today need to be ____ **(3.)** and ____ **(4.)** in order to understand the challenges faced by workers. Bosses that remain ____ **(5.)**, locking themselves away in the office, are less effective. Thomson also said that ____ **(6.)** leaders who regularly work 18-hour days are disappearing. His other theme was decision-making. Leaders who ____ **(7.)** in the face of problems are not real leaders, while those who remain ____ **(8.)** while under pressure are.

1. **a.** a gravitas **b.** an inspiring **c.** an aloof
2. **a.** nondescript **b.** dignity **c.** charismatic
3. **a.** corrupt **b.** approached **c.** approachable
4. **a.** down-to-earth **b.** charisma **c.** lacking in energy
5. **a.** inspirational **b.** idealistic **c.** aloof
6. **a.** trustworthy **b.** tireless **c.** tiring
7. **a.** wave **b.** drive **c.** waver
8. **a.** powerful **b.** resolute **c.** trusted

UNIT 7
The natural world

LESSON 1

Reading

1a Read the article below. Then answer the questions.

1. What do Jiggs, Bart, Rock of Gibraltar and Keela have in common?
____
____
2. Why might the chief of the South Yorkshire Police Force be jealous of Keela?
____
____
3. What do the police use Keela for?
____
____
4. What were the FBI interested in?
____
____

The dog with the golden nose

(1) Jiggs, the chimpanzee who starred in over fifteen Tarzan movies in the 1930s, was paid thousands of dollars. The owner of Bart, an Alaskan brown bear, was paid a million dollars for letting Bart appear in the film *The Edge*. A racehorse called Rock of Gibraltar is worth an estimated $170 million. And now there is Keela, a dog doing a great job and getting well remunerated for it.

(2) The spaniel is no movie star, but she has become so important for South Yorkshire Police in England, that she now earns more than the chief of police. The secret of her success? Keela has an astonishing sense of smell. She can sniff traces of blood on weapons that have been scrubbed clean after attacks and even on clothes that have been washed repeatedly in biological laundry detergent. PC Ellis, Keela's handler, said, "She can detect minute quantities of blood that cannot be seen with the human eye. She is used at crime scenes where someone has tried to clean it up."

(3) Once they realized Keela had these extraordinary skills, the dog handlers used a special training regimen to hone her talent. In fact, her training was so successful that the FBI has inquired about it.

(4) Not surprisingly, Keela is in demand with other crime-busters. For her services, other police forces are charged $850 a day, plus expenses. She earns the South Yorkshire Police Force around $320,000 a year, more than PC Hughes, her boss! Hughes says there are no hard feelings. "Keela's training gives the police force an edge when it comes to forensic investigation which we should recognize and use more often."

b Find words in the article that mean:

1. paid for a job or service (*v.*) (paragraph 1) _______________
2. very small amounts of something (*n.*) (paragraph 2) _______________
3. cleaned (by rubbing it) (*v.*) (paragraph 2) _______________
4. extremely small (*adj.*) (paragraph 2) _______________
5. to improve a skill so that it is done very well (*v.*) (paragraph 3) _______________
6. no angry thoughts (three words, idiomatic) (paragraph 4) _______________

c Cover the article. Match a word from A to a word from B to make phrases from the text.

A			
chief	training	crime	sense
movie	laundry	dog	in

B			
star	of police	of smell	detergent
scene	handlers	regimen	demand

d Complete the summary of the article. Use the phrases you made in Exercise 1c.

She may not be a _______________ (1.) like other high-earning animals, but Keela is similarly _______________ (2.). She has an incredible _______________ (3.); she can detect blood even after clothes have been washed in _______________ (4.). This makes her especially useful at a _______________ (5.). Once the _______________ (6.) realized she was so exceptional, they invented a special _______________ (7.) for her. She now makes more money than the _______________ (8.)!

Grammar

2 Circle the correct word or phrase to complete each sentence.

1. Jan wants to eat at Bob's Kitchen or King Curry House, ____ appeals to me.
   a. neither which **c.** neither of which
   b. of neither which
2. I met the writer Kate Atkinson, ____ books made such an impression on me.
   a. of which **b.** whose **c.** with whose
3. The lead actor, ____ the show depended, didn't turn up.
   a. who on **b.** on whom **c.** who
4. Carrie left early, ____ seems strange to me since she usually loves parties.
   a. that **b.** which **c.** who
5. Zadie, ____ five children are brilliant mathematicians, is no good at math.
   a. of whose **b.** who's **c.** whose
6. The party leader, ____ asked to justify himself, could not.
   a. when **b.** who **c.** while

3 Complete the sentences using ideas from the box, plus *who*, *when*, *which*, or *whom*. You may need to add a preposition.

Ex: There were a hundred guests, most *of whom I'd already met.*

know/the way	I/buy/yesterday
eat/all/chocolate	be/interested
work OK/now	~~meet/ already~~
brother/work/with my wife	

1. It was Juan ________________. That's why he's feeling sick!
2. When I was lost, I asked four people, none ________________.
3. These books, ________________, got really great reviews.
4. Last week, we fixed these computers, all ________________.
5. This form must be completed before the conference. Please check the topic in ________________.
6. I spoke to the woman ________________.

Vocabulary

4 One word in each sentence belongs in another sentence. Find the words and cross them out. Then write them in the correct sentences.

1. By watching the movements of animals, we can predict natural safety, such as earthquakes and tidal waves.
2. There are many stories of drowning people being carried to instincts by dolphins; these may be true because dolphins rescue animals the same size as themselves.
3. Animal disasters often allow animals to escape from danger that humans don't notice.
4. Rescue teams work with dogs because of the dogs' excellent invisible of smell.
5. Birds used to save sense during wartime by carrying vital messages to army commanders.
6. In the dark, cats and bats see things that are lives to the human eye.

5 Complete the article by adding words from the box.

tricky	once	this	step	if
straightforward	put	need	of	

Teaching a parrot to talk

Bird expert Olaf Sund says that teaching a parrot to talk is a piece cake. Here, he gives a few invaluable tips.

The first thing you to do is choose the right bird. Bigger birds, like Blue Fronts and Yellow Napes, are your best bet, and make sure you get them when they are young. Birds older than 18 months probably won't learn to talk.

You've chosen the bird, put it in the room where the family congregates the most—maybe the living room. For parrots to learn how to talk, human interaction is the key.

At first, it can be a little for any wild animal in a domestic environment, so give the bird a few weeks to acclimate. The next is to turn off the TV and remove any distractions. Place the bird on your hand and say a word in conjunction with an action or object. For example, give it a peanut and say: "Peanut" or lift the bird up and say: "Up." The process must be pretty, so use short, simple words at first.

Be gentle and patient with the bird, and lots of emotion in your voice. Teach the bird in 15-minute sessions, and give rewards, such as food, when the bird repeats a word. Without doing, some birds are slow to speak. Your teaching doesn't work, you should allow another family member to try. Many birds prefer a female voice.

LESSON 2

Reading

1a Read the three excerpts from *Extreme Landscapes* on the right. Write questions for the answers.

1. ______________________________?
   Because they know where the water is.
2. ______________________________?
   Because, by looking at them, you will see how the landscape has changed over millions of years.
3. ______________________________?
   Like a person or animal roaring.
4. ______________________________?
   Behind the water, next to the rock face.
5. ______________________________?
   Captain Cook's.
6. ______________________________?
   60,000 years old.
7. ______________________________?
   Because a coral reef is actually alive.

b Answer the questions on a separate sheet of paper.

Death Valley

1. Why does the writer mention a man frying an egg on a car?
2. Why do you think he says "You grow a new skin?"

The Iguaçu Falls

3. What images connected with the voice does the writer use to describe the Iguaçu Falls?
4. Why does he "wonder if [the birds] can ever hear themselves sing?"

The Great Barrier Reef

5. The writer calls the Great Barrier Reef "a million jewels." What do you think he means?

c Find words in the excerpts that mean:

1. burning brightly (excerpt 1) ____________
2. crawl desperately, with your face to the ground (excerpt 1) ____________
3. an enormous hole in the surface of the earth (excerpt 2) ____________
4. forced into a small space (excerpt 2) ____________
5. waterfall (excerpt 2) ____________
6. crashed (excerpt 3) ____________
7. long pieces of heavy wood used in buildings and ships (excerpt 3) ____________
8. clear, transparent, allowing light to pass through (excerpt 3) ____________

The Great Barrier Reef

The Iguaçu Falls

Death Valley

1: Death Valley

Don't get me wrong. I've seen a man fry an egg on the hood of his car in Arizona. I've seen birds drop dead out of the sky from the heat. I've seen acres of cracked Sudanese earth and the jawbone of a wildebeest fifty miles from the nearest water. But nothing can prepare you for Death Valley in the depths of a blazing summer. Everywhere you look, the air is shaking like fire. You grovel for water, following the trails of wise animals, keeping your distance. You grow a new skin, like leather.

The joy of Death Valley is in the rocks. Look closely and you'll see the history of the world. Burned into those rocks are the stories of climate change, the mutations of wind, water, and gravity since the beginning of time.

2: The Iguaçu Falls

What hits you first is the sound. Long before you get close, you hear the roaring, like some great giant's endless breath. As you approach, it gets louder, until finally you see it—a vast chasm beyond your imagining, endless tongues of screaming white water and spray rebounding a hundred feet into the air. The Iguaçu Falls. I look over the edge and I see behind the water, jammed against the rock, birds' nests! A whole colony of them. They made their home in the middle of the world's biggest cataract. And now, twisting like corkscrews from under the spray, the birds rise free into the air and float above us. I wonder if they can ever hear themselves sing.

3: The Great Barrier Reef

In 1770, Captain Cook's boat rammed smack into the reef. A barrel of rum fell overboard and sank. Little did he know that underneath the wooden beams of his ship there was a world of such magnificence, such translucent light and life. The Great Barrier Reef is a million jewels. Flatback turtles and humpback whales, dolphins and clownfish and giant clams with sprawling shells. The Great Barrier Reef is a poem to itself: 1,243 miles (2,000 kilometers) long and 60,000 years old, 900 islands and 3,000 coral reefs. They say you can see it from space.

I duck beneath the water for the twentieth time, the scuba tank heavy on my back. I am still trying to believe my eyes. The water is like a glass kaleidoscope, a riot of color. This is the biggest living organism in the world, and I am swimming in its blue heart.

Grammar

2 Match each sentence or phrase to the statement that could follow it.

1\. ____ 1. She remembers talking to Joe.
____ 2. She remembered to talk to Joe.
a. At the last party she accidentally ignored him.
b. They were outside the library.

2\. ____ 1. I regret telling you about the accident.
____ 2. I regret to tell you about the accident.
a. I should have kept it a secret.
b. Fortunately, nobody has been seriously hurt.

3\. ____ 1. Huan tried drinking the special remedy,
____ 2. Huan tried to drink the special remedy,
a. but he couldn't swallow it because it was so disgusting.
b. but it didn't cure him of his illness.

4\. ____ 1. The old man stopped listening to the birds.
____ 2. The old man stopped to listen to the birds.
a. They were singing beautifully so he stayed there for a while.
b. They were making such a terrible noise that he couldn't stand it any more.

5\. ____ 1. Since the children liked his first game,
____ 2. After buying his first Lego set at the age of eight,
a. he continued inventing games all afternoon until everyone had had enough.
b. he went on to invent lots of games, and eventually he became famous.

3 Complete the story below using the correct form of words from the box.

experience	travel	make	go
become	leave	take	stay

Life choices

She remembered ____________ **(1.)** that photo. It was the first day of her trip in the desert. While her friends were content to sit on a beach during their vacations, she always tried ____________ **(2.)** new customs, new places, new people. She used to say, "The day I stop ____________ **(3.)** the world is the day I die." Her parents thought she would go on ____________ **(4.)** either a travel writer or a tour guide, but instead, one day, she just never returned.

On a trip to Egypt, she had stopped ____________ **(5.)** for a camel ride near the Pyramids in Cairo. She had never meant ____________ **(6.)** longer than a day or two, but as she watched the sun slowly falling over the sand dunes, casting them in a sea of orange, she fell in love with the desert and vowed to stay. It meant ____________ **(7.)** behind the safe world that she had known all her life, but now, 40 years later, sitting at her home in Alexandria, looking over the photos, it was a choice she has never regretted ____________ **(8.)**.

Vocabulary

4 Match the beginning of each sentence with its end.

____ 1. Fish River Canyon probably has the most spectacular
____ 2. I thought Siberia would have been too cold for permanent
____ 3. Disneyland is one of the world's most visited tourist
____ 4. There are a number of active
____ 5. Death Valley in California is 282 feet below
____ 6. Many places in Arkansas became ghost
____ 7. I like Rio's vibrant

a. volcanoes in Italy, including Mount Vesuvius.
b. towns after a terrible epidemic killed 70,000 people.
c. landscape in Africa. It's the world's second biggest canyon.
d. nightlife. There's always a party going on somewhere.
e. settlement, but there are large communities that live there.
f. sites—millions see it every year.
g. sea level.

Grammar

1 Match the questions to the answers.

____ 1. How many pictures should we take?
____ 2. Who's going to be there?
____ 3. What do the expensive tickets cost?
____ 4. How far is it to Jacksonville?
____ 5. Do you go there regularly?
____ 6. What have you heard about me?
____ 7. How tall is he?
____ 8. Can I have some of your water?

a. Yes, as much as you like.
b. Over $100.
c. Virtually everyone.
d. Virtually nothing.
e. Well, less than ten miles.
f. Approximately six feet.
g. As many as we can.
h. As often as possible.

2 Circle the word or phrase that could be or should be added to the sentence.

1. I'm told that all of them passed—only two people had to retake the exam.
   a. majority c. virtually
   b. precisely
2. Our classes cost $224.99 per week, an absolute bargain!
   a. as much as c. as little as
   b. as many as
3. Your suitcase weighs 50 pounds, which is the limit!
   a. well over c. a minimum
   b. much above
4. This elevator takes ten people.
   a. a majority of c. virtually
   b. a maximum of
5. A people wanted Jones to win, but everyone else voted for Smith.
   a. small majority c. few of
   b. tiny minority of
6. During the winter, we sometimes get two or three tourist groups a week.
   a. as little as c. as few as
   b. a great deal of
7. I need 123 of those bottles. No more, no less!
   a. precisely c. a minimum of
   b. approximately

Vocabulary

3 Each monolog has two mistakes. Find the mistakes and correct them.

1. "Well, yes, it's used, but it's in great condition. This really is a rare opportunity because it's a latest model, as I'm sure you realize. Everything's in working order, although I haven't tried the brakes yet. And don't worry about that tear and wear on the tires. They'll be fine."

2. "This one is a very rare opal stone. It really is one in a kind. Over a thousand years ago, it was probably worn by a tribal queen. Despite its age, you can see that it is in perfect conditions."

3. "This model has only been on the markets for a few weeks and it's unbelievable; you've got wide-screen vision, anti-reflection technology, and it even features an intelligent remote control that knows your viewing tastes. It's absolutely state-in-the-art and it's yours, brand new, for just $10,000."

4. "OK, OK, they're second-hand but they're as well as new. I mean, look, they're still in the original packaging! They come in a wide arrangement of colors and sizes, and the lenses are just fantastic. What do you mean, 'the sun's not going to come out'?"

5. "These are all made to hand. We pick the fruit in the morning, chop it up and coat it in sugar and honey. Then, we roll the pastry and put the fruit inside it. You can choose from a selecting of over fifteen fruits."

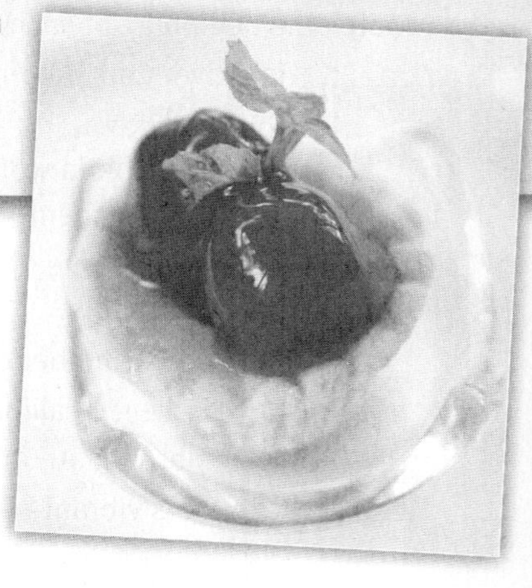

Writing

4 Choose one of the pictures below. Imagine you are selling the item(s) online. Write the ad on a separate sheet of paper.

Communication

5a Read the statements. Check the response that best describes your view.

1. Scientists should be banned from doing medical experiments on animals.

   1 = agree completely ☐ 2 = it depends ☐ 3 = disagree completely ☐

2. People who mistreat their pets should go to prison.

   1 = agree completely ☐ 2 = it depends ☐ 3 = disagree completely ☐

3. Animals should not be put in circuses or used for other forms of entertainment.

   1 = agree completely ☐ 2 = it depends ☐ 3 = disagree completely ☐

b Read the interviews on the right. For each interview, answer the following questions. Use a separate sheet of paper.

1. What is his or her job?
2. Has the speaker (or his or her profession) been criticized? If so, what for?
3. Does the speaker justify this treatment of animals? If so, how?
4. How does the interviewer feel about the issue? How do we know?

Ethical dilemmas

Interview 1

A: Jennifer, you say your profession is under attack, but isn't it the mice, the monkeys, and the other animals, that are suffering?

B: I realize the ethics of it aren't simple, but to have people burning down labs and threatening the families of scientists is something else entirely.

A: Three million experiments on animals were conducted in the US alone last year, in the name of science. How can we possibly justify those sorts of numbers?

B: Well, first, I would dispute those figures. But the main point is that the experiments are for the benefit of humankind. Without them, we'd be much worse off. No one wants to harm an animal intentionally, but you have to weigh a number of issues.

Interview 2

A: Heather, you've written, and I'm quoting here, that you "see the darker side of humanity every day." Can you explain what you mean by that?

C: Well, I work for the Humane Society, a charity that protects animals. I go wherever there are abuses of animals, and some of the things I see are very shocking.

A: Could you give us an example?

C: I could give you thousands. A week ago, I discovered that a family had locked up a large dog in a four-by-four-foot cupboard for one week, without giving it food or water. So, that's what I mean by the darker side of humanity.

A: It seems impossible in this day and age that these things can still happen, doesn't it?

Interview 3

D: It had always been one of the great traditions of our circus, but eventually the pressure became too great.

A: And that's why you stopped using animals?

D: For myself, and a number of other circus managers, it was obvious that times had changed. But it wasn't an easy decision to get rid of animals from our act.

A: What effects has the decision had?

D: Well, the first thing was that I had to fire about 50 members of the staff whose job was taking care of or training the animals, and that was very tough for them and me. The second thing was that little children would come to the circus expecting to see monkeys and elephants and sea lions, and they wouldn't be there.

A: Do you believe it was wrong to use the animals in the circus, when we know they were taken from their natural environment and basically captured and trained to entertain people?

D: No. The animals were treated extremely well. It was pressure from outside that forced the decision on me.

UNIT 7
Review

1 Find words in Unit 7 of the Student Book that match the definitions. The first letter is given.

1. a__________ = many medical scientists do ____ *testing* before testing medicines on humans (*n.*)
2. b__________ = animals do this to have offspring (*v.*) OR particular type in a species of animal (*n.*)
3. c__________ = meat eater (*n.*)
4. d__________ = animal that can smell a bomb (*n.*)
5. e__________ = ____ *species* are types of animal which may become extinct soon (*adj.*)
6. f__________ = *the* ____ *trade* uses precious animal skin for clothing (*n.*)
7. h__________ = an animal's ____ is the place where wild animals live (*n.*)
8. h__________ = when humans pursue and kill an animal for food (*v.*)
9. i__________ = animal ____ allow animals to sense danger (*n.*)
10. l__________ = an expanse of land seen from one view point (*n.*)
11. m__________ = animal that feeds its young with milk from its body (e.g. cows, humans) (*n.*)
12. o__________ = when humans catch too many fish in one place, leading to changes in the ecosystem (*v.*)
13. p__________ = any animal that hunts another (*n.*)
14. r__________ = a *nature* ____ is an area of land where wild animals are protected (*n.*)
15. s__________ = area for birds or animals where they are safe and can't be hunted (*n.*)
16. v__________ = you and your pet may need one to avoid diseases (*n.*)
17. w__________ = spider's home OR where you can buy animals illegally (*n.*)

2 Circle the phrase to finish each sentence. Both choices may be correct.

1. I went to greet the children, some ____.
   a. of whom I'd already met
   b. of them I'd already met
2. We visited the two proposed sites, ____.
   a. of which neither was appropriate
   b. neither of which was appropriate
3. I went bowling last night, ____.
   a. that was enjoyable
   b. which was enjoyable
4. That's the multinational corporation ____.
   a. for which she worked
   b. which she worked for
5. That's the singer ____.
   a. whose CD you're always playing
   b. who's CD you're always playing
6. There must be a hundred lights in here, ____.
   a. none of them work
   b. none of which work
7. We are walking the same path ____.
   a. that Robert Frost walked
   b. which Robert Frost walked
8. This is one law ____.
   a. which we all benefit from
   b. from which we all benefit
9. It's a profession ____.
   a. in that I hope to succeed
   b. in which I hope to succeed
10. The stadium was full of people, ____.
   a. most of whom supported Brazil
   b. most of which supported Brazil

3 Circle the best words below to complete the article.

Earthquake!

Ten minutes after the earthquake struck, the ____ (1.) ran into the remains of the building, which was located close to a ____ (2.). They were there to ____ (3.). Again and again they removed huge chunks of brick and carried the injured people ____ (4.). They didn't normally deal with ____ (5.) like earthquakes. The dangers they ____ (6.) were usually due to human error — people getting trapped in elevators and things like that — but it didn't ____ (7.) to them. Lives were lives. When it seemed as if there was no more to be done, one of the men sensed a movement, something almost ____ (8.) the human eye. They had combed every inch of the building, but the man's ____ (9.) going in there. Within minutes he emerged carrying a tiny cat. The cat's ____ (10.) had told it to hide under a cupboard, where it had subsequently become trapped.

1. a. rescuing team
   b. rescue squad
   c. rescue team
2. a. tourist site
   b. touristic area
   c. tourism site
3. a. safe lives
   b. be saved lives
   c. save lives
4. a. safely
   b. to safety
   c. for safety
5. a. nature disasters
   b. nature's disasters
   c. natural disasters
6. a. faced
   b. touched
   c. made
7. a. make the difference
   b. mean any difference
   c. make any difference
8. a. invisible to
   b. invisible for
   c. invisible with
9. a. heart was decided on
   b. heart was set on
   c. head was set on
10. a. animal's instinct
    b. intelligent instincts
    c. animal instincts

4 Finish the words to complete each sentence.

1. We found that a large m________ of people (nearly 90%) wanted to change their job.
2. V________ none (0.3 %) of the people felt that they would be in the same job for the rest of their lives.
3. A small m________ (around 3%) said they had applied for a new job in the last month.
4. As f________ as 13% of participants claimed that they would like to go (back) to school.
5. Most of the participants had been in work for ap________ ten to fifteen years.
6. 30% said their salary is w________ u________ what they deserve, and want more money.
7. 60% believe they will be in their current job for a mi________ of two more years.

5a Match the beginning of the sentence with its end.

____	1. It's in	a. wide range of colors.
____	2. It's as	b. by hand.
____	3. It's the	c. of-the-art.
____	4. It's state-	d. new.
____	5. It's on	e. of a kind.
____	6. It's made	f. the market.
____	7. It's one	g. wear and tear.
____	8. It has some	h. good as new.
____	9. It comes in a	i. latest model.
____	10. It's brand	j. excellent condition.

b Find expressions in Exercise 5a that mean:

1. You can choose from a selection.
   ____
2. It's handcrafted.
   ____
3. It's still in the original package.
   ____
4. It's unique.
   ____
5. It's available now.
   ____

6a Put the words in the correct order to make sentences.

____ 1. breaking/up/tricky/a/fight/can/dog/very/be
____

____ 2. if/hit/will/it/you/you/dog,/attack/the
____

____ 3. the/next/to/do/walk/dog/is/to/thing/you/the/backwards/have
____

____ 4. finally,/from/the/away/dogs/other/each/tie
____

____ 5. second,/help/get
____

____ 6. first,/hit/dog/the/don't
____

____ 7. once/you/dog's/the/help,/grab/hind/legs/have
____

b Number the sentences in the correct order.

UNIT 8
Problems and issues

LESSON 1
Communication

1a Read the interview on the right and choose the best summary.

The interview describes ____.

a. problems we will have in the future and possible technological solutions

b. some new inventions that may help people in the future

c. ways in which technology has improved the lives of ordinary people

b Read the interview again. Mark the statements true (*T*) or false (*F*).

____ 1. V2V involves cars "talking to each other" through a computer system.

____ 2. The new cell phone will tell you how nervous or confident you look.

____ 3. The new cell phone was invented to help people during "speed dates."

____ 4. The memory device is not just one machine.

____ 5. According to Gordon Bell, recording your life is rather boring.

c Write the words from the box in the correct category.

squeaky	gadget	unintelligible
gizmo	swerve	hand-held device
sensor	pedal	backseat driver
		steering wheel

driving	
technology	
the voice	

Future world

A: What do you have for us, Barry?

B: Well, we have an amazing selection of gadgets and gizmos for the future, including a car that can't crash, and a cell phone that tells you "you're never going to get a date if you talk like that!" And some software that will allow you to carry years and years of memories in your pocket. How about that?

A: Sounds terrifying.

B: It isn't.

A: So, tell us about the car. What is it and how does it work?

B: We're entering James Bond territory here. The system is called V2V. It stands for "vehicle to vehicle communication." Basically, we're talking about sensors on the side of the road that will exchange information with your car about what other cars are doing. Not only that, but the car will also swerve to avoid a crash. We're talking about a backseat driver, but one that's always right!

A: That's great. Sounds like a lifesaver.

B: It is. They're even working on steering wheels that can shake sleepy drivers awake and pedals that vibrate.

A: Fantastic. What about the cell phone?

B: Well, this is a different kind of lifesaver. It's going to be a big help to shy young men trying to get a date.

A: How's that?

B: It's a socially-aware cell phone that can analyze voice patterns and tell you if you sound nervous or cool. It can tell you if you're speaking too fast, or if you're unintelligible, or even if your voice is too squeaky! It was recently piloted at a speed dating session and the participants loved it!

A: Very interesting. What about the memory device?

B: It's actually a few devices: a mini-camera that can fit into a contact lens and a microphone that fits in your ear. You download the data onto a hand-held device and there you have it: a lifetime's worth of memories.

A: But who would want it?

B: Gordon Bell.

A: Who's he?

B: A researcher who's been recording his entire life, since 1998, for a project called MyLifeBits.

A: Wow.

B: He scans all of his photos and documents, and records meetings, phone calls and emails, and he wears a mini-camera round his neck to get an image of everything he sees.

A: But isn't it unbelievably boring?

B: Well, according to Bell, it's not. He says it's similar to having an assistant with a perfect memory. But I imagine it depends on just how boring your life is.

Vocabulary

2 Complete the paragraphs with words from the box.

overrated	waste	live
underrated	benefits	

In my view, cell phones are ____________ (1.). They are not a complete ____________ (2.) of space, but we don't really need them. In the past, we just made arrangements more carefully or used pay phones.

We can't ____________ (3.) without cell phones. They have huge ____________ (4.) for society because they allow us to communicate more, which is a great thing. I actually think they are ____________ (5.); we don't realize how useful cell phones are until we find ourselves in an emergency.

Grammar

3 Circle the correct words or phrases to complete the sentences. Two choices may be possible.

1. She ____ to college, but he just wanted to find a job.
   a. insisted Ben going
   b. encouraged Ben to go
   c. suggested that Ben go
2. Morger ____ the money.
   a. warned us to steal
   b. denied stealing
   c. threatened to steal
3. Claudia ____ eating the cake, even though I was innocent.
   a. accused me of
   b. threatened to
   c. blamed me for
4. I ____ I had been stupid.
   a. admitted that
   b. confessed that
   c. informed that
5. Ling ____ take our warm clothes.
   a. encouraged that we
   b. told us to
   c. reminded us to
6. He always ____ his record was the best.
   a. accused that
   b. maintained that
   c. insisted on

4 Rewrite each sentence using the correct form of the verb in parentheses.

1. Mr. Anderson told us again to read the safety precautions. (remind)
   Mr. Anderson ______________________________.
2. "My advice is to call a doctor," said Lena. (suggest)
   Lena ______________________________.
3. We had taken it for granted that you knew each other. (assume)
   We ______________________________.
4. She said Tom had stolen the apple. (accuse)
   She ______________________________.
5. We had to say that we didn't know the answer. (admit)
   We ______________________________.
6. I said "well done" to her for passing her exam. (congratulate)
   I ______________________________.
7. Dad said he'd withhold our allowance if we continue to behave badly. (threaten)
   Dad ______________________________.
8. "I've never met her before!" said Young-soo. (deny)
   Young-soo ______________________________.

5 First put the letters in parentheses in the correct order to make a word. Then, put the words in the correct order to anwer the question.

1. **A:** So, what will you do next?
   B: (nusqoiet) ____________/a/that's/good
   ____
2. **A:** Which of your co-stars was your favorite?
   B: (lelw), ____________/I/of/all/them/loved
   ____
3. **A:** Of all your movies, which would you like to be remembered for?
   B: (tel) ____________/see/me
   ____
4. **A:** Do you regret starring in any of your movies?
   B: (ikhnt) ____________/I'd/that/about/to/have
   ____
5. **A:** Will you get married again for a sixth time?
   B: (rkctyi) ____________/that's
   ____
6. **A:** Who was your favorite director?
   B: (iitfcldfu) ____________/question/that's/a
   ____

LESSON 2

Vocabulary

1 Complete the sentences with words from the box.

security	out	hair	buzz	and

1. Because of stress and high expectations, many tennis players burn ____________ before they reach 30.
2. A lot of business people who are already rich and successful say that the main motivator is no longer money, but the ____________ and excitement of making deals.
3. Mark was tearing his ____________ out with frustration when they overlooked him for a promotion again.
4. Julie tries to save some money every week as a ____________ blanket in case of unexpected disasters!
5. I don't think work should come before family; your career isn't the be-all ____________ end-all.

Grammar

2 Match the questions to the answers.

____ 1. Why did she look so sad?
____ 2. Why did they look tired?
____ 3. Why are they such a mess?
____ 4. Why did the police stop him?
____ 5. What were all those people doing there?
____ 6. When did Brian start his trip?
____ 7. Why isn't Anna Rita taking the class?
____ 8. What were all those secret meetings about?
____ 9. Why didn't Suyin answer the phone?
____ 10. What's she doing in that room?

a. They were being taken on a tour of the harbor.
b. They'd been talking all night.
c. They'd been thinking of selling the company.
d. I think she's been playing computer games all evening.
e. She may have been sleeping when you called.
f. He'll have been traveling for exactly two weeks this time tomorrow.
g. He must have been driving too fast.
h. She was going to a funeral.
i. She's expecting a baby in one month!
j. They've been painting the window frames.

3 Complete the story using the correct form of the verbs in parentheses. Use the continuous form of the verb if possible.

My 92-year-old great aunt is called "Dutchie," but that's just a family nickname. My grandmother says that Dutchie's real name is Adulcia—or at least that's what she thinks. My grandmother says that she never heard her sister called by her real name, so she's not even sure how to pronounce it. As a child, my great aunt could never pronounce it either, and her attempts always sounded like "Dutchie," so the name stuck.

Dutchie ____________ (**1.** live) with us in New York City right now. She has never been in a big city before. In fact, until this year she ____________ (**2.** never/be) more than 50 miles from the small town in Vermont where she was born. However, even though she had seen very little of the world, she ____________ (**3.** gather) a lot of wisdom throughout her life.

My great aunt and I have always been close. I lived with her the summer after I graduated from college. I'll always remember our first morning together that summer. When I woke up, it ____________ (**4.** rain) hard. I felt as bad as the weather outside. At that time, I ____________ (**5.** have) a lot of problems with my parents, who wanted me to attend medical school. I ____________ (**6.** struggle) to convince them that I wasn't cut out to be a doctor. The sight of blood actually made me ill and I ____________ (**7.** hate) studying. Dutchie ____________ (**8.** sense) right away that something was wrong. We had a long talk that morning, as the rain lashed the windows and drummed on the roof. Dutchie took my hands in hers and looked deep into my eyes. Her advice to me was simple: "Choose a job that you love, and you'll never work a day in your life." I've ____________ (**9.** follow) her advice for over 30 years, and I've never regretted it.

Reading

4a Read the ideas. Check them once if you already do them. Check twice if you would like to try them.

20 ways to beat stress

____ 1. **Learn something new, such as a sport, a language, or a skill, like painting. Short bursts of intense concentration are a great way to relieve stress.**

____ 2. Teach yourself massage techniques, yoga, or t'ai chi.

____ 3. **Make the most of seasonal fruits, such as strawberries, raspberries and cherries. They are full of feel-good nutrients.**

____ 4. Pamper yourself once a week: watch a movie, have a soothing bath with oils, or buy yourself a bouquet of your favorite flowers.

____ 5. **Write down something good that happened to you in each year of your life.**

____ 6. Avoid sugary snacks and sodas that are likely to give you a temporary high. Drink water and snack on natural foods, such as nuts, instead.

____ 7. **Call up your inner child, and do something you haven't done for years, like playing on a swing or putting on an old pair of roller skates.**

____ 8. Talk to someone about your problems. Bottling things up only makes them worse.

____ 9. **If you have a sedentary job, do something physical like gardening or going for a run.**

____ 10. Switch off every machine in the house, ignore all but the most urgent emails for 24 hours, get comfortable, and read a book.

____ 11. **Bake bread. Kneading dough is hard work, but soothing, and the smell of fresh bread is guaranteed to lift your spirits.**

____ 12. Get back to nature. Treat yourself to a long walk in a park.

____ 13. **Meditate. Cultivate optimistic thoughts. Think of what you have, not what you want.**

____ 14. Get rid of all the clutter on your desk. Throw away everything you don't really need.

____ 15. **Look through your wardrobe. If you haven't worn something for over 18 months, give it to a charity, or to someone who will wear it.**

____ 16. Go to a karaoke bar and sing away your worries. Alternatively, close all the doors, put on your favorite music at full volume, and sing or dance until you're exhausted.

____ 17. **Go to bed an hour earlier than usual to improve your sleep.**

____ 18. Cut down on alcohol, nicotine, and caffeine. Reduce your intake gradually, and you may find that you can give it up altogether.

____ 19. **Go home a different way. For instance, walk home from work if it's not too far.**

____ 20. Eat at least one meal a day with friends or family.

b Find words in the article that mean:

1. sudden periods of activity or noise (*n.*) (suggestion 1) ____________
2. give someone lots of loving care and attention (e.g., buy them gifts, etc.) (*v.*) (suggestion 4) ____________
3. makes you feel calm and less worried (*adj.*) (suggestion 4) ____________
4. a feeling of having lots of energy or great happiness (*n.*) (suggestion 6) ____________
5. not allow yourself to show feelings (*v. + prep.*) (suggestion 8) ____________
6. involving sitting down and not moving (*adj.*) (suggestion 9) ____________
7. work hard to help something grow (*v.*) (suggestion 13) ____________
8. things that fill space untidily and aren't necessary (*n.*) (suggestion 14) ____________

c Complete the sentences using the correct form of the words in Exercise 4b.

1. I hated my ____________ lifestyle, stuck behind a desk for eight hours a day, so I took up jogging.
2. Loretta went for a ____________ massage every morning.
3. Don't ____________ your problems. Tell me about them.
4. We need to remove useless ____________ from our lives and to focus on what is essential.
5. My husband really ____________ me. He buys me flowers and new clothes every week.
6. She's very good at ____________ personal relationships. She writes letters, invites people to dinner, and always keeps in touch.
7. Caffeine gives you a temporary ____________, but you shouldn't have too much of it.
8. I completed all my work in a two-day ____________ of energy!

Communication

1 Read five phone messages. For each message, answer the following questions. Use a separate sheet of paper.

a. What exactly is the problem?

b. What must the receiver of the message do?

Message 1
Hi Joseph, it's Chris. Just wanted to say that something's come up and, basically, I'm not going to be able to make it to your place by six, so I'll try and get there, well, as soon as I can. It's a problem with the air conditioning here at the office, and basically the only time the maintenance guy can come is after 5:30, so I have to stay a few minutes late. Anyway, I'll be there as soon as possible. Bye.

Message 2
Hello, it's Sandy from Small World Travel. There's a problem with your tickets to Fiji. Can you give me a call at (555) 249-0312. Thank you.

Message 3
Hello, honey, it's me. If you get this message, can you try and get in touch with Monica about babysitting? I completely forgot to ask her yesterday, and I don't have her phone number on me. We need her from about seven until twelve tomorrow. Talk to you later.

Message 4
Hello. My name is Alexandra Duvall, and I bought a Classic Body Toner Home Gym from you on Saturday. It was delivered on Monday, but there seems to be a problem with it. Right now, I can't get the machine to work at all, even though the guys who delivered it said it was easy, and I've followed the instructions in the manual. Could you please send a mechanic over as soon as possible—I really need to get it working immediately. My customer order number is 675637. Thank you.

Message 5
James, this is Liz Jordan. I just got the message that our keynote speaker is sick and won't be able to come to the conference, so it's pretty urgent that we find a replacement. I haven't talked to William yet, so could you please pass on this message. And give me a call. You can reach me on my cell any time. Bye.

Grammar

2 Circle the correct choice.

http://www.great_advice.com/marriageconcerns.html

Great_advice.com

My fiancée and I are planning our wedding. The matter/worrying/thing (**1.**) is, we want a small, informal one (family and best friends only), but we don't want to offend people by not inviting them. The fact to the matter/remains/of the matter (**2.**) is, they all invited us to their weddings, and we feel a little bit mean having a private one. **Alex**

Alex, I understand your concerns, but the matter/point/trouble (**3.**) is, it's your special day, and it's for you to decide how you want to spend it. Ignore all other considerations. **Sajid**

Hi, Alex, one thing you could/option you/way to (**4.**) do is organize a party for all your friends a few weeks before you get married, and explain to them that you want a quiet wedding. **Sue**

http://www.happy_to_help.com/marriageconcerns.html

Happy_to_help.com

My husband's son from his first marriage still lives at home, although he is 23. The thing irritates/The matter for/What irritates (**5.**) me is that he doesn't work or study, and he does nothing around the house, treating me like a servant. My husband keeps saying "give him time," but my patience is running out. What we need/What needs/The matter (**6.**) to do is talk to him seriously about the situation, but my husband refuses. **Georgia**

Dear Georgia, although your husband's attitude is, in some ways, understandable, the fact stays/remains that/remains (**7.**) he needs to take the lead in this situation. He must talk to the boy. **Kerry**

Georgia, what could happen/what you could try/the trouble (**8.**) is to set some rules about housework; and draw up a schedule that everyone has to follow. **Joanne**

Vocabulary

3 Circle the correct choices to complete the article.

As anyone who's ever waited in a long line will testify, there's nothing like bad service to kill a business. It can also be a *major source/big root/serious consequence* (**1.**) of stress when something goes wrong and no one seems willing to help. We've heard stories of people waiting on the phone for an hour before customer service picks up, or people hanging on for weeks to get faulty equipment replaced. The *stem/result/cause* (**2.**) is that customers will go elsewhere next time, and also tell others their horror stories. Mark Bradley wrote a book called *Inconvenience Stores* about a year of customer service in the UK. The idea *had it origins in/was originated in/was original in* (**3.**) some research Bradley was doing for a business presentation, but the fascinating anecdotes *result in/had a result that/resulted in* (**4.**) increased interest, and eventually he wrote a whole book. It doesn't make for happy reading. At one point, he asks for a latte and is told "You'll have to go to Leeds (another city) for that." He concludes that much of the poor service *has its origins/origins/gives rise* (**5.**) in the fact that employees have no power to make decisions. In one hotel chain, employees have to get permission to say no to customers. Naturally, this *consequences/causes of/leads to* (**6.**) serious problems for the hotel. So, how can businesses *reach/bring about/breed* (**7.**) change in the form of better service? Bradley thinks that companies need to improve morale among employees and give them the freedom to do what's right for the customer. The *source/consequences/origins* (**8.**) could be wonderful for us all!

4 Complete the conversations by adding words from the box.

appears	won't	get
turning	showing	seem

1. **A:** I'm having problems on the oven.
   B: Yes, there's something wrong with it.
2. **A:** I can't the washing machine to wash the clothes.
   B: That's because it's a dryer!
3. **A:** The computer doesn't to be working.
   B: That's because you haven't turned it on.
4. **A:** The car still start.
   B: Let's call the mechanic.
5. **A:** The clock is always the wrong time.
   B: I know. It needs a new battery.
6. **A:** This light to be broken. It doesn't turn on.
   B: I think the bulb's burned out.

Writing

5a Read the opening lines of this essay. Number the sentences in the correct order to complete the essay.

Procrastination affects most of us at some time or another. For this reason, a number of studies have been carried out looking into its causes and consequences. Furthermore, we have tried to develop and evaluate a number of possible solutions to the problem.

____ Consequently, putting it off just adds to that feeling of anxiety, because time is running out.

__1__ The first cause we discovered was a lack of concentration.

____ For example, some perfectionists believe they must do extensive research before writing anything.

____ Instead of dealing with the task at hand, many people let their mind wander, staring out of the window or surfing the net.

____ This means that they read and read but never actually get around to writing the paper.

____ A third cause is perfectionism.

____ The second cause was fear; when we are worried that a task is beyond us, we tend to put it off.

b Underline useful linking and sequencing expressions. The first two have been done.

UNIT 8 Review

1a Read the excerpt from a story. Which person was most frightened? ______________________

"Don't go in there," said June. But they were determined to go. Mike, the oldest, said, "Why should we listen to you anyway? You're just a kid!"

"It's haunted!" replied June. "And if you go in there, I'll tell my mother!" Mike just laughed and said, "You're lying." But Sally was nervous.

"What if June's right?" she asked. Mike said, "Don't be ridiculous. Ghosts don't exist. We'll be out of there in two minutes."

"OK," said Sally. As they approached the house, June ran the other way and shouted, "Don't forget what happened to the dog!"

"Thanks!" said Mike, as he grabbed Sally's hand and stepped through the doorway. At that moment, their lives changed, and nothing would ever be the same again.

b Read the excerpt again and complete the sentences. Use the words in parentheses when they are given.

1. June warned ______________________. (the house)
2. June claimed ______________________.
3. June threatened ______________________.
4. Mike accused ______________________.
5. Mike informed ______________________. (ghosts)
6. Mike persuaded ______________________. (go in)
7. Sally agreed ______________________. (the house)
8. June reminded ______________________.

2 Circle the correct words or phrases to complete the sentences.

1. The book is not nearly as interesting as I thought it would be. It's a little ____.
   a. underrated
   b. overrated
   c. indispensable
2. The new banking laws have ____.
   a. had big benefits for us
   b. made big benefits for us
   c. benefit us
3. All this technology isn't really necessary. We ____.
   a. can't do without it
   b. can do without
   c. can do without it
4. That building is hideous, and it serves no purpose. What ____!
   a. a space waste
   b. a waste of space
   c. a waster of space

3 Match the beginning of each sentence with its end.

1. ____ 1. We've built a tree house, which
   ____ 2. We've been building a tree house, which
   a. we're hoping to finish tomorrow.
   b. the children play in every day.

2. ____ 1. He might have been voting
   ____ 2. He might have voted
   a. this morning, which would explain why he wasn't here.
   b. for an independent candidate in the last election, but I doubt it.

3. ____ 1. Dana was being taught Chinese
   ____ 2. Dana was taught Chinese
   a. the last time I saw her.
   b. when she was a child.

4. ____ 1. We'll have been studying
   ____ 2. We'll have studied
   a. this verb form six times if we do this lesson.
   b. here for exactly two years by this time on Monday.

5. ____ 1. It's raining
   ____ 2. It rains
   a. between June and September.
   b. again.

6. ____ 1. I've been seeing her
   ____ 2. I've seen her
   a. in the same place, at the same convention, every year since 1982!
   b. before.

4 Seven of these items have an extra word. Cross out the extra words and check the correct sentences.

1. Behaviorist theory has its own roots in an experiment by Ivan Pavlov. ______
2. His research was to have far-reaching and consequences for psychology. ______
3. When Pavlov placed meat powder on a dog's tongue, the dog salivated. ______
4. Pavlov then began ringing a bell just before giving the dog the meat powder. ______
5. This resulted but in the dog salivating when it heard the bell, even if it ______
6. didn't get any meat powder afterwards. Many psychologists concluded that by ______
7. a major source of motivation is conditioning. This had a huge influence so ______
8. on many areas of life, including language learning. For example, ______
9. behaviorist theory gave a rise to the audiolingual method (listen and repeat). ______
10. It also brought us about many changes in the teaching materials used. ______

5 Rewrite each sentence using the words in parentheses.

1. I'm fed up with all that noise. (thing/irritates)

____

____

2. My main concern is the cost involved. (what/ worries)

____

____

3. To tell the truth, I'm tired of this game. (fact)

____

____

4. There are too many people; that's the problem. (trouble/is)

____

____

5. He broke his promise. There's nothing we can do to change that. (fact/remains)

____

____

6. The house is in good condition. That's the important thing. (point/is)

____

____

6 Each conversation has one mistake. Find the mistakes and correct them.

1. **A:** This toaster keeps to burn the toast.
   B: Well, why don't you buy a new one?
2. **A:** I can't get this door to close. Can you help me?
   B: Let me to see.
3. **A:** Can you give me a hand tomorrow? I'm having problems finishing all this work.
   B: I'll have to think of that. I'm pretty busy myself.
4. **A:** My car can't start. What can I do?
   B: That's a difficult question.
5. **A:** This drawer seems to be too stuck. How does it open?
   B: That's a good question.

UNIT 9
People with vision

LESSON 1

Vocabulary

1 Complete the puzzle and find the key word.

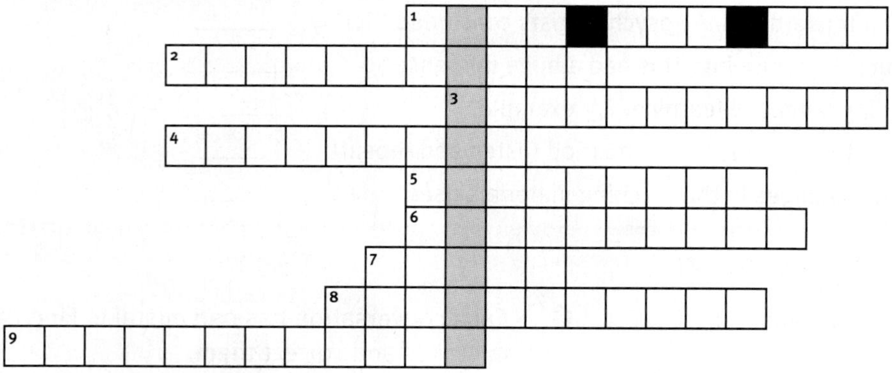

1. It was funny to watch although the acting was really ____.
2. The Mona Lisa is a ____.
3. It was a beautiful opera and the scenery was just ____.
4. The town is full of ____ architecture.
5. The artist's ____ of the royal family are well-known.
6. The special effects in the new *Star Wars* movie are ____.
7. It's a long book about the history of nuclear physics, so it's a very ____ read.
8. Unfortunately, the characters are rather ____.
9. I'm really into ____ art these days.

Grammar

2 Circle the correct prepositions. Who is the artist?

Perhaps one of the most tragic masters of art, this painter yearned _for/on/to_ (**1.**) recognition during his lifetime, but was denied it until after his death. He is universally seen as one of the greatest artists _at/in/of_ (**2.**) all time.

To/On/For (**3.**) one occasion, he said of his paintings: "I cannot help it if my paintings do not sell. But the time will come when people will realize that they are worth more than the cost of the paint." His vision was correct. This artist was an indisputable genius, who was also undeniably ignored. He became famous _for/of/at_ (**4.**) the hundreds of bold, bright paintings he produced, many of which have become some of the best known, paintings of the 20th century, but only one of which was ever sold during his lifetime. The work he specialized _at/in/on_ (**5.**) was avant-garde _in/for/of_ (**6.**) his time, and as such, was not accepted by the general public.

He spent the latter part of his life absorbed _in/on/at_ (**7.**) his work. However, he was always _over/in/under_ (**8.**) stress, and suffered _for/from/of_ (**9.**) depression. It is now thought that epilepsy may have contributed _to/with/in_ (**10.**) the psychological breakdowns that plagued him until his untimely death.

Reading

3a Read the biography on page 69. Then choose the correct answers.

1. Why is Stephen Hawking so famous?
   a. Because he has researched time travel.
   b. Because of his ideas and his physical condition.
   c. Because he is unable to speak.
2. Stephen suffers from a rare disease that
   a. has left him in a vegetative state.
   b. means he can talk unaided but he cannot move.
   c. makes both speech and movement almost impossible.
3. His physical condition has
   a. meant that he never enjoyed a family life.
   b. probably contributed to his fame.
   c. impeded him from achieving greatness in his professional career.

Stephen Hawking: Triumph of a Mind over Matter

1 Stephen Hawking is undeniably one of the world's most gifted and revered scientists. His groundbreaking contributions to the study of the universe and the nature of space and time have electrified the scientific world. Moreover, his public appearances and best-selling books, in which he explains his theories to general readers, have made him an international celebrity. His achievements are even more remarkable given his severe physical handicaps: Hawking has a rare disease called amyotrophic lateral sclerosis (ALS), a condition that gradually left him almost completely paralyzed and unable to speak. The story of how Hawking overcame the limitations of his disease and continued his scientific work is nothing short of remarkable.

2 Hawking was born in Oxford, England, on January 8, 1942, into a distinguished family. His mother had been one of the first women to be accepted to Oxford University. His father, also an Oxford graduate, was a respected medical researcher. Meals at the Hawking home were usually eaten in silence, with each member of the family engrossed in a book. After supper, the Hawkings would often lie in the backyard and gaze up at the stars. Hawking's mother recalls, "Stephen always had a strong sense of wonder. And I could see that the stars would draw him."

3 Although he was recognized as being very intelligent, Hawking did not put much effort into his schoolwork. Instead, he busied himself with personal projects, inventing board games and building a primitive computer out of recycled parts that could solve basic math problems. Despite his lack of focus in the classroom, Hawking graduated with honors from Oxford University in 1962, with a degree in natural science, and went on to Cambridge to do research in cosmology.

4 It was at this time that Hawking began to exhibit his first symptoms of ALS. He started to trip and fall down and had difficulty speaking clearly. After a series of tests, doctors made a grave diagnosis: the nerves controlling his muscles had begun shutting down. They predicted that Hawking would have only a couple of years to live. He refused to allow the devastating news to crush his spirit. In fact, Hawking found he began to enjoy life as never before. He asked a fellow student named Jane Wilde to marry him, and she accepted. He began to make progress with his research and won a fellowship at Gonville and Caius College, Cambridge. Hawking and Wilde married in 1965 and had three children together. As Hawking's body deteriorated, his mind soared to new heights. In 1974, he amazed the scientific community by using quantum theory and general relativity to demonstrate that black holes can emit radiation. The next year, he published his first book, *Large Scale Structure of Space Time*. In 1979, Hawking was named Lucasian Professor of Mathematics at Cambridge, a great honor for someone so young.

5 However, Hawking's physical condition worsened. Confined to a wheelchair since 1969, he gradually lost the ability to perform basic tasks, such as feeding himself and getting in and out of bed. In 1985, pneumonia robbed him of the ability to speak. Refusing to give up his work, Hawking learned to use a speaking program that he directed with a sensor attached to his cheek muscles. It allowed him to select words on a computer screen that were then "spoken" by an electronic speech synthesizer. Using this system, Hawking wrote *A Brief History of Time* in 1988, an easy-to-understand explanation of the workings of the universe that has sold over 25 million copies worldwide. Other books and important discoveries followed and secured Hawking's reputation as the preeminent theoretical physicist in the world. Today one of the longest-lived and most productive survivors of ALS, Hawking continues to write at a prolific rate and remains dedicated to finding the answers to science's biggest mystery: the explanation of how the universe began.

b Find words or phrases in the article that mean:

_____________ 1. much admired (*adj.*) (paragrah 1)

_____________ 2. new and radically different (*adj.*) (paragraph 1)

_____________ 3. make people very excited (*v.*) (paragraph 1)

_____________ 4. completely interested in something (*v.*) (paragraph 2)

_____________ 5. very simple, basic (*adj.*) (paragraph 3)

_____________ 6. seriously bad (*adj.*) (paragraph 4)

_____________ 7. the best of its kind (*adj.*) (paragraph 5)

c On a separate sheet of paper, rewrite this summary. Correct the mistakes.

Stephen Hawking was born in London, England in 1942. A hard-working student, Hawking spent all of his time in the classroom. Since he was a small child, Hawkins suffered from a disease known as ALS. Doctors predicted that he would only have a couple of months to live. However, Hawking refused to give up hope. He continued his research and married Jane Wilde in 1979. Hawking discovered new information about earthquakes that surprised the scientific world. His first book, *A Brief History of Time*, was published in 1988. These and other accomplishments have cemented his reputation as one of the greatest scientists of all time.

LESSON 2

Vocabulary

1 Put the letters in parentheses in the correct order to make words to complete the sentences.

1. I like ____________ paintings best, especially ones by artists like Kandinsky and Mirò. (scatbart)
2. It's very ____________. You can't help but notice it when you walk into the room. (tigrnski)
3. His techniques were very ____________ for the time. (navat-draeg)
4. Her still life paintings are ____________ and simple. (lacm)
5. The landscapes are very ____________ and relaxing to look at. (nailqurt)
6. He is famous for his ____________ portraits. (lorcoluf)
7. I found the sculptures of dead animals highly ____________. (tirgsubind)
8. It's a masterpiece. Absolutely ____________! (racpeslatcu)
9. Their earlier works were more ____________ in style. (ladanotirit)
10. Some people love them, but personally I find landscapes a little ____________. (ludl)

2 Complete the conversations by adding words from the box.

admired	my	into	relate
all-time	fan	cup	kind

1. **A:** Did you like the dress?
   B: I'm sorry, it's just not my of thing at all.
2. **A:** What do you think of the decor?
   B: It's really not taste.
3. **A:** Did you enjoy Seiko's latest exhibition?
   B: Yes. I'm really her work.
4. **A:** How about this one? Do you like the style?
   B: It's not really my of tea.
5. **A:** Have you heard the new Rihanna album?
   B: I'm not a big of her stuff.
6. **A:** *Twilight* is on TV tonight.
   B: Great. It's an favorite of mine.
7. **A:** Ali Smith won an award for her latest novel.
   B: She deserved to. I've always her work.
8. **A:** What do you think of the exhibition?
   B: I just can't to this kind of thing.

Grammar

3 Use the words in parentheses to complete the sentences.

Ex: As I was saying, I'm going to talk to you about education.

1. I can ____________ see what you mean. (sort)
2. ____________, I haven't really understood what you are talking about. (honest)
3. ____________, I would rather stay at home and watch a movie. (truth)
4. We can ____________ be sure that they intend to buy. (more)
5. ____________, we should be able to get a good price. (rate)
6. ____________, I wouldn't want to stay there on my own. (mind)
7. ____________, I think the ideas should be discussed at a meeting. (matter, fact)
8. ____________, it is the best offer we are going to get. (far, concerned)
9. ____________ when we should leave, I don't think it makes any difference. (for)
10. ____________, they proved us wrong in the end. (fact)
11. ____________ changing the policy completely, I'm not in a position to answer. (regarding)

Vocabulary

4 Complete the sentences with words from the box.

hideout	undercover	stuffed	haul
tracked	mastermind	chainsaw	crack

1. He is suspected of being the ____________ behind the bombings.
2. The man was discovered in a ____________ in the woods.
3. He worked ____________ in Colombia and Panama.
4. Detectives finally ____________ her down in California.
5. She quickly ____________ two more sweaters into her bag.
6. They used a ____________ to cut through the heavy doors.
7. This new evidence could help detectives to ____________ the case.
8. The gang escaped with a ____________ worth hundreds of dollars.

Reading

5a Read the article and choose the best title.

a. A Good Deal **b.** Momentarily Fooled **c.** Texan Rebel

(1) In 1952, Elmyr de Hory returned to Los Angeles after a prosperous sojourn in Dallas, Texas. He had managed to sell some of his stash of alleged masterpieces, including some Picasso and Matisse drawings. He had made a huge profit and was hoping he would be equally successful in Southern California. Elmyr had set up an appointment with art dealer Frank Perls, owner of a well-known Beverly Hills gallery, and he planned to unload more of his artwork for another sizeable profit.

(2) Elmyr dressed in his best suit for the occasion, carrying with him a large portfolio. At his meeting with Perls, Elmyr presented what he claimed were drawings he'd inherited from his family following World War II. The portfolio purportedly included sketches from Picasso, Matisse, Renoir and Modigliani.

(3) Perls took one look at the work and was immensely impressed. After all, it's not often that one has the chance to hold great masterpieces by some of the world's most famous artists. However, the longer Perls looked at the pictures, the more concerned he became. It was clear that something was wrong, and Perls' worrisome expression discomforted Elymr.

(4) According to Clifford Irving's book, *Fake!,* Perls questioned Elmyr about his address and other detailed personal information, causing Elmyr to become nervous. Perls then calmly placed the pictures back into the portfolio, tied the strings, and then suddenly threw them at Elmyr. Elmyr was shocked by the unexpected action, and was uncertain what to do next, until Perls ordered him to get out.

(5) Elmyr then walked out of the gallery with Perls yelling behind him. Perls observed what an untrained eye would likely never notice: these works were fakes. It was also true that they were created masterfully.

(6) To Perls' surprise, Elmyr asked him, after being thrown out of the gallery, whether he thought the drawings were well done. According to Irving, Perls replied: "They certainly fooled me for a few minutes," before ordering the counterfeiter away again. The incident was not Elmyr's first or last time at trying to sell excellent forgeries. In fact, he had been doing it successfully for years.

(7) Unbeknownst to Frank Perls, Elmyr had sold some forgeries to Perls' brother, Klaus, in New York several years earlier. Elmyr's involvement with the two Perls brothers would later cause unexpected problems. In fact, one of the Perls brothers would be directly involved in what would later be the end of Elmyr's career as a skillful art forger.

(8) For approximately three decades, Elmyr de Hory used his extraordinary talent to reproduce masterpieces from some of the world's greatest artists, including Picasso, Vlaminck, Chagall, Toulouse-Lautrec, Dufy, Derain, Matisse, Degas, Bonnard, Laurencin, and Modigliani. His accuracy for detail fooled even the most skilled art connoisseurs into believing that his creations were authentic. Given their alleged provenance, Elmyr sold his forgeries for high prices. Moreover, he managed to elude Interpol and the FBI for most of his criminal career.

(9) Elmyr de Hory eventually became known worldwide as one of the most talented art forgers in history. Even after his death, Elmyr's works still attracted attention. Some of them even sold for the same prices as the originals. Like many famous painters, however, he died penniless, after a series of unfortunate events.

b Read the article again. Mark the statements true (*T*) or false (*F*).

____ 1. Elmyr de Hory traveled to Dallas with just a couple of paintings.

____ 2. He sold paintings for a small profit to art dealers.

____ 3. Perls immediately spotted Elmyr as a fake by the way he was dressed.

____ 4. Elmyr made up stories about the origins of the paintings.

____ 5. Perls' questions worried Elmyr.

____ 6. Elmyr had been successfully selling fake paintings for about 30 years.

____ 7. He had been chased constantly by the FBI and Interpol.

c Figure out the meaning of the words. Use the context of the article to help you.

1. prosperous (paragraph 1) ____________
2. stash (paragraph 1) ____________
3. purportedly (paragraph 2) ____________
4. worrisome (paragraph 3) ____________
5. masterfully (paragraph 5) ____________
6. forgeries (paragraph 7) ____________
7. fooled (paragraph 8) ____________
8. elude (paragraph 8) ____________

LESSON 3

Vocabulary

1 Complete the conversation with words from the box.

out of focus	disposable	close-up
foreground	accessories	flash
vacation shots	digital	

Julia: Do you want to come and see my ______________ (1.) of Thailand?

Kasem: Sure.

Julia: That's me in the ______________ (2.). Behind me is the Royal Palace. This one's a little ______________ (3.). You can't see it very clearly.

Kasem: But most of these are great pictures. Did you use a ______________ (4.) camera?

Julia: No, just a cheap little ______________ (5.) camera. I threw it away after the vacation.

Kasem: So it didn't have any ______________ (6.) like a tripod or anything?

Julia: No way! I prefer to keep it simple. This one's a little dark. We took it at night and I don't think the ______________ (7.) was working.

Kasem: Wow! Who's this, taking up the whole frame?!

Julia: This is a ______________ (8.) of my aunt. You can see every pore in her skin!

Grammar

2 Match the beginning of the sentence with its end.

____ **1.** I wish I hadn't
____ **2.** I wish I
____ **3.** If only they
____ **4.** It's about
____ **5.** It's high time
____ **6.** I'd rather you didn't put
____ **7.** What if you hadn't
____ **8.** Suppose I could

a. time you got a haircut.
b. your feet on the furniture.
c. been wearing a seat belt?
d. were here now.
e. offer you a bonus?
f. we had a little talk.
g. bought that car.
h. could play the guitar.

3 Rewrite each sentence using the word in parentheses.

1. Rashid lost his passport, so he couldn't board the plane. (only)
   If ______________________________.
2. You're acting like a child and you should stop! (high)
   It's ______________________________.
3. We really should get back to work now. (about)
   It's ______________________________.
4. Can you imagine being offered that job? Would you accept? (if)
   What ______________________________?
5. What will happen if we press this button? (suppose)
   ______________________________?
6. Lucia is an only child, but she wants a baby sister. (wish)
   Lucia ______________________________.
7. What did you want to do last night: go out or watch a DVD? (rather)
   Would ______________________________?

4 On a separate sheet of paper, put the words in the correct order to answer the questions.

1. What if the board asked you to become chairman of the company?
   it's/agree/highly/I'd/likely
2. Suppose they stopped you illegally? What would you do?
   I/taking/consider/them/court/definitely/to/would
3. If she asked you, would you lend her ten thousand dollars?
   it's/to/I'd/able/be/that/do/unlikely/that
4. You're not thinking of dropping out of the class, are you?
   there's/I/do/way/that/would/no
5. What if we offered you half of our winnings?
   I/agree/probably/that/to/would
6. Would you be willing to coach the team for free?
   I/that/I/might/suppose/doing/consider

Communication

5a Read the interview with a photographer. Answer the questions on a separate sheet of paper.

1. How did her family influence her choice of career?
2. What did she like about her first camera?
3. Why does she take different types of photos?
4. What type of pictures is she taking these days?
5. What "has its own sort of visual vocabulary" and what do you think she means by this?

b Complete the summary. Read the interview again to check your answers.

> Sandrine started by taking photos of __________ (1.) in her __________ (2.) garden at the age of __________ (3.). She now photographs many things, including nature and famous __________ (4.). She thinks a photographer's job is to capture __________ (5.) and __________ (6.). She says she is interested in __________ (7.). Sandrine lives near a __________ (8.) and loves to photograph the light there.

c Find the phrases in the interview. Match them to the definitions.

____ 1. what distinguishes you from
____ 2. your incredibly diverse output
____ 3. a restless soul
____ 4. being pigeonholed
____ 5. feeling a little bit peeved
____ 6. at the end of the lens
____ 7. every subject under the sun
____ 8. a sense of awe

a. as the subject of a photo
b. being forced to fit into a category
c. what makes you different
d. all the topics that exist
e. a feeling of wonder because something is amazing or beyond normal life
f. someone who can't stay still or stay in the same place
g. feeling annoyed
h. the things you produce that are in a very wide range of styles

A PHOTOGRAPHER'S MEMORIES

I: Sandrine, can you tell us a bit about how you got started as a photographer?

S: It all goes back to my grandmother, actually. She lived in Colombia as a child, and when she moved back to West Virginia, she insisted on planting tropical flowers in this tiny back garden of hers because they reminded her of her childhood. Whenever the flowers bloomed, the colors were astonishing. On my tenth birthday, my father gave me a Polaroid camera and I started taking pictures of grandma's garden. And the beauty of the Polaroid was that you didn't have to send the pictures away to be developed. They just slipped out of the bottom of the camera in all their glory.

I: From pictures of grandma's garden to celebrities, landscapes, underwater photography, and even social realism. What distinguishes you from other photographers is your incredibly diverse output. The product of a restless soul, perhaps?

S: You could say that. I dislike being pigeonholed. I remember reading an article about contemporary photographers a few years ago, which described me as "Sandrine Kafer, the celebrity photographer," and I remember feeling a little bit peeved that that was how some journalist saw me. I'd always thought of myself as a photographer pure and simple, whose job is to capture a moment of truth and beauty. Whether it's a famous person at the end of the lens, or two little boys on a bicycle, or soldiers, or life at the bottom of the ocean, in many ways it's the same thing to me.

I: So this diversity hasn't been a conscious career decision?

S: Not really, no. I just take opportunities where I find them, and I suppose, above all, I'm interested in everything. I have a library of about 6,000 books at home, very few of them on photography, and they cover every subject under the sun. And once you start getting interested in something, you want to see it and find the truth in it, and then, of course, if you're a photographer, you want to capture it on film.

I: Your recent work seems less crowded, perhaps more tranquil than anything you've done before.

S: Well, I live on 20 acres of land with a river close by, and birds and animals. The light is stunning, and it always amazes me that the river can look like this at five in the morning, and like that at midday, and different again at dusk. Actually, whenever you work with water, there is a sense of awe. It's where life began. It has its own rhythm and its own sort of visual vocabulary.

UNIT 9 Review

1a Add the correct prepositions.

1. devoted his life ____________
2. the development ____________
3. ____________ the field (e.g., of physics)
4. be famous ____________ (something)
5. immersed ____________
6. specializes ____________
7. succeed ____________
8. ____________ several occasions
9. in recognition ____________
10. draw inspiration ____________
11. (one of the best) ____________ all time

b On a separate sheet of paper, rewrite the sentences that contain phrases in bold. Use the phrases from Exercise 1a.

Hi, Arline,

How are you? Everything's fine here at Los Alamos. You wouldn't believe some of the scientists I'm working with. There's Hans Vogel, who ***is focusing on*** particle theory. He has really ***given everything of himself to*** his research. He's probably one of the greatest scientists ***in history***. There's also Bernheimer, ***renowned for*** his work in physics. He won the Nobel Prize for his contribution to nanotechnology. He's the world's greatest expert ***in his area***. He is totally ***focused on*** his work, which is ***the creation and production of*** a new type of weapon. I've managed to speak to him ***a few times***, and even though he's working in very tough conditions, he doesn't seem to feel the stress.

I've been able to ***get motivated through*** my contact with these people, and I really hope I can ***do well in*** my work here.

Love,

Richard

2 Ten words are missing. Add them to complete the conversations.

1. **A:** Didn't you just love that movie?
   B: As matter of fact, we thought it was a little boring.
2. **A:** Be honest, I don't like ballet much.
   B: Far as the skill is concerned I think it's wonderful, but I can't say I've seen much of it.
3. **A:** Isn't that CD wonderful?
   B: To tell you truth, I think it's a bit overrated.
4. **A:** That movie was kind long, wasn't it?
   B: Long? I fell asleep at least twice. It was endless!
5. **A:** Bye, Hiro! Anyway, Rosa, I was saying, that restaurant is fantastic.
   B: Mind, it's not exactly cheap.
6. **A:** So if you can get three tickets, that'd be great.
   B: Any rate, I'll get at least two, OK?
7. **A:** He wrote, directed, and starred in that play.
   B: Frankly, he more less did everything!
8. **A:** Sorry, Keith. I interrupted you.
   B: I was going to say was that I enjoyed the exhibition very much.

3 Circle the correct choices to complete the paragraph.

Most companies, on making a mistake, publicly deny it and privately say, "Oh, no! If only we *have/had/should have* (1.) done this!" Venture capitalists, who help fund new businesses, spend half their lives wishing they *have poured/must have put/had poured* (2.) money into one thing and not another. Not Bessemer Venture Partners. This company has an "anti-portfolio" website which lists the great opportunities they missed. The list contains some of the biggest names in business. *If only/Should/What if* (3.) Bessemer had put money into an unknown company called Apple Computers? *Suppose/Supposed/Wishing* (4.) they hadn't turned down eBay? At the time eBay sold stamps and comic books, and Bessemer didn't see the potential. If only they *must have been/had been/had be* (5.) able to read the future! Bessemer also turned down Google before it was famous. So why does Bessemer admit these mistakes? According to the website, they *would rather/are rather/rather* (6.) laugh at their errors than try to cover them up. It may also be a marketing ploy; new businesses *had rather/prefer/would rather* (7.) go to a venture company that has a reputation for honesty and openness than one that doesn't. Our conclusion? It's *the right time/high time/the time* (8.) other companies came out and admitted (or even laughed at) their own mistakes.

4 Put the letters in parentheses in the correct order to complete the paragraph.

Jackson Pollock's early paintings were __________ (**1.** fgitareivu), though never realistic. In the 1940s, his work became more __________ (**2.** asttacrb) and less __________ (**3.** tdaanilorit), until he reached his zenith in the drip paintings of the mid-1940s. These were truly __________ (**4.** vatan-rgdae), __________ (**5.** stgninnu) works, painted on a huge scale. Although critics called Pollock a barbarian because of his technique, and found the violence of both his life and work __________ (**6.** dibgsrniut), what is __________ (**7.** stgrniki) about Hans Namuth's documentary of him painting is that he seems completely __________ (**8.** tqnaiurl) as he dances around the canvas, dripping paint.

5 Cross out the ending that is NOT possible.

1. That type of art isn't _____.
   a. my kind of thing
   b. my cup of tea
   c. my liking
2. It became clear that the facts in the case were _____.
   a. indisputable
   b. without a doubt
   c. undeniable
3. Bearing in mind the circumstances, I _____.
   a. would consider to do that
   b. would agree to that
   c. suppose I might agree
4. That's what they say, but in my opinion, it's _____.
   a. questionable
   b. debatable
   c. unquestionably
5. People think he reached the North Pole, but it's not _____.
   a. 100% certain
   b. without a doubt
   c. clear-cut
6. Her paintings weren't universally popular, but the critic Herman Bowers was _____.
   a. a big favorite
   b. really into her work
   c. a big fan
7. Daniel is worried that I'm going to leave the company, but _____.
   a. there's no way I'd do that
   b. I wouldn't probably do that
   c. it's unlikely I'd be able to do that
8. Some people hated those art-house movies, but Mrs. Williams _____.
   a. really related to that type of thing
   b. had always admired them
   c. couldn't agree to them

UNIT 10

Expressing feelings

LESSON 1

Vocabulary

1 Read what five people say about their feelings. Then write a sentence to summarize how each person is feeling. Use phrases from the box.

down in the dumps	of two minds
pleased with herself	wound up
at her wits end	

1. ______________________________

2. ______________________________

3. ______________________________

4. ______________________________

5. ______________________________

2 On a separate sheet of paper, write a response to each person in Exercise 1.

Just a feeling . . .

1 I'm not really enjoying my job right now, and I don't seem to have much time to go out either, so I don't feel like I'm really making the most of life. I often don't get home until 9:00 or so, and it's too late to cook, so I usually end up just eating cereal in front of the TV and then falling asleep. And then before I know it, it's time to go back to work again.

2 I can't understand why she hasn't called me yet. I mean, she said she would call as soon as she arrived, and it's been two days now. I can't help thinking that something must have happened. It's not like her to not even send a text message. I'm worried sick. I'm going to have to call the police.

3 It's a boy! We went to have the tests yesterday, and I'm so excited. I can't believe you can actually see the baby on the screen, with his little hands and feet and everything. I have a photo of him, and it is the most amazing feeling. I used to be afraid to be a mother, but I'm so proud of myself for making this decision. I can't believe how happy I am, and to think that in just a few months . . .

4 I can't believe it. It is so annoying. I have waited all this time to get an appointment with a specialist, months and months, and now they write a letter to say that that specialist can't treat me anyway, and I need to find someone else. I mean, why didn't they just say that before, six months ago?! We pay huge amounts of money to these doctors, and it makes me so angry when you can't even get a simple appointment.

5 I'm not really sure what I want to do. I could come just for the day, I suppose, but it's such a long trip that I don't know if it's worth it to drive all that way. On the other hand, it would be great to see you all again, and if I don't come now, I don't know when I'll have another chance. And it's been so long since we saw each other . . .

Grammar

3 Rewrite the sentences using the words in parentheses.

1. It wasn't really necessary for us to bring all this equipment. (need)

 ____

 ____

2. There is a good chance that they'll find out sooner or later. (bound)

 ____

 ____

3. I think it would be a good idea if we looked around the house first. (ought)

 ____

 ____

4. She will probably do well in the race. (likely)

 ____

 ____

5. I can't believe there is no easier way to do this. (must)

 ____

 ____

6. I've asked her a hundred times already, but she is refusing to change her position. (won't)

 ____

 ____

7. It's impossible for them to charge that much for a service. It's ridiculous. (can't)

 ____

 ____

8. It's likely that we'll bump into you at the party on Saturday. (might)

 ____

 ____

9. They ask you to take your shoes off before you go in. (supposed)

 ____

 ____

4 Circle the correct words to complete the sentences.

1. Tim's flight took over fifteen hours. He ____ be exhausted.
 a. is supposed to **b.** is likely **c.** must
2. If you don't speak Mandarin, you ____ accept the job.
 a. can't **b.** are supposed **c.** are bound
3. Nobody ____ to talk in the library.
 a. is bound **b.** is supposed **c.** can't
4. He's had the problem for weeks, but he ____ see a doctor.
 a. ought **b.** won't **c.** is likely
5. The housing office ____ to help you find somewhere to live.
 a. ought **b.** can't **c.** might
6. You didn't ____ to have it delivered. I could have picked it up myself.
 a. ought **b.** might **c.** need

Vocabulary

5 Complete the ad with words or phrases from the box.

tough times	work out	dwelling
challenges	outlook	optimistic
chances are	looking on the bright side	

Would you say that you tend to be more ________________ (1.) or more pessimistic? When you go through ________________ (2.), do you usually assume that things will ________________ (3.) in the long run, or do you take a more negative view? If you think that you need a little help ________________ (4.) and would like to work on thinking more positively, a new class at the Wellness Center might be just the thing for you.

Our class will help you adjust your ________________ (5.) on life, helping you to see the positives in situations, rather than the negatives. We will lead you through exercises designed to make you aware of your thought patterns. We will help you to look for solutions to problems instead of ________________ (6.) on the negative aspects of a situation. ________________ (7.), when you have completed our class, you will be much more likely to see your problems as ________________ (8.) to be overcome, and you will have a healthier way of looking at your life.

LESSON 2

Grammar

1 Rewrite each sentence using the word in parentheses.

1. It's impossible for it to have been Pete in that car. (can't)

 ____

 ____

2. There's no answer. Maybe they've gone to bed. (could)

 ____

 ____

3. You weren't looking where you were going. The car nearly killed you. (might)

 ____

 ____

4. I'm not sure that they're still in the city. I think they moved. (may)

 ____

 ____

5. I'm glad you came. It would have been impossible without you. (couldn't)

 ____

 ____

6. I can't find it anywhere, but I know it's here. (must)

 ____

 ____

7. Rick and June are undecided about whether to come to the wedding reception. (might)

 ____

 ____

8. Someone called and left a message. It's possible that it was Carmen. (may)

 ____

 ____

9. I can't believe you are serious. (must)

 ____

 ____

10. They're still not here. Maybe they got lost. (might)

 ____

 ____

Vocabulary

2 Put the letters in parentheses in the correct order to make adjectives to complete the sentences.

1. He was ______________ about being asked to play in the band. (ldrihtel)
2. Her family are ______________ about her name being published in the newspaper. (soruifu)
3. Emma was a little ______________ by his directness. (kante bacak)
4. The people lining the streets were ______________ when they caught sight of the celebrities. (citsceta)
5. Tiffany was absolutely ______________ to him, and it hurt. (dirntfenief)
6. She's been so ______________ since Patrick left her. (silermabe)
7. He was ______________ in politics. (terenuetinsd)
8. Sid is ______________ of heights. (frerietid)
9. When I found out how much money we'd made, I was absolutely ______________. (blastabfredge)
10. When we heard the news we were ______________. (scmurktudb)
11. Customers were ______________ by the price increases. (tuadroge)
12. Sandy will be ______________ to see you. (lehtdideg)
13. She was absolutely ______________ that he had lied. (divil)
14. I'm ______________ of spiders. (diterfipe)
15. She was really ______________ about the way her father treated her. (spute)

Reading

3 Read the article on the next page. Check the feelings and emotions that are described.

___ anger	___ boredom
___ ecstasy	___ hurt
___ contentment	___ frustration
___ fear	___ jealousy
___ regret	___ surprise

Revenge Can Be Bittersweet

(1) **Lady Sarah Graham-Moon became a hero to jilted women everywhere when she became famous for gettting even with her unfaithful husband.**

(2) According to Lady Sarah Graham-Moon, her second husband, Sir Peter Graham-Moon, had been unfaithful for years, but events came to a head in 1992, when he moved his girlfriend into the neighborhood in which they lived in Berkshire, in the south of England. Having been angry about his behavior for years, Graham-Moon planned her revenge carefully.

(3) For starters, she poured gallons of white paint on his BMW and cut the sleeves off 32 of his custom-made Savile Row suits, which cost approximately $1,600 each. She also cut up several of his pricey cashmere coats. She then deposited 60 bottles of rare wine from his extensive collection on the doorsteps of many of their neighbors.

(4) Lady Moon became an instant celebrity. She appeared on the Oprah Winfrey Show, wrote a column for a national British newspaper, wrote a book on getting even with unfaithful spouses, and started a club, called the Old Bags Club, to support women who had been abandoned by their husbands. Moon insists that the goal of the club is not to counsel revenge, though she believes that revenge, if not taken too far, can be therapeutic. The main goal of the club, she says is to help women regain their self-esteem and self-reliance. The women who dwell on the details of the unfaithfulness are the ones who need the most help, she says. "They keep on hating the guy, and it does them more harm than him."

(5) Moon and her unfaithful husband got divorced, and she later found happiness living with David Denyer, a gamekeeper whom she met in the mid-1990s. Accustomed to aristocratic men like her ex-husband, Moon was pleasantly surprised by how straightforward, honest, and decent Denyer was. Though they had been raised in completely different circumstances, Moon and Denyer found that they were somehow very compatible. They lived together in her home and raised chickens and hunting dogs. Moon recalls that it was the first time that she had been truly happy.

(6) Unfortunately, Moon's happiness was not to last. In February 2006, Denyer died in a shooting incident. Though some experts thought it to be suicide, Moon strongly disagreed. "If David had wanted to kill himself, he would have done it properly," she was quoted as saying. She believes that he fell, causing his gun to go off accidently.

(7) Moon's one regret? Not marrying Denyer. He had asked her to, but she had said no, having already gone through two failed marriages. Though she is again on her own, Moon credits Denyer with restoring her self-confidence. She clearly misses him very much. Her eyes well slightly with tears as she discusses him but, like a true English aristocrat, she holds her emotions in check. "Death is all around us," she says. "It isn't very nice, but there's no use crying great crocodile tears."

4 Read the article again. Mark the statements true (*T*) or false (*F*).

____ **1.** Lady Sarah Moon felt happiness for the first time when she met her third husband, David.

____ **2.** Moon's second husband was unfaithful to her.

____ **3.** Moon destroyed her husband's expensive clothes.

____ **4.** She destroyed his expensive bottles of wine.

____ **5.** Moon and Denyer had similar childhoods.

____ **6.** Moon started a club to teach other women how to get revenge.

____ **7.** Moon disagrees with some experts on the cause of Denyer's death.

____ **8.** Moon has no regrets.

5 Would you have reacted similarly to Lady Sarah Moon if you had been in a similar situation? Explain your answer.

____

____

____

____

____

____

____

____

____

____

____

____

____

____

____

LESSON 3

Reading

1a Read the excerpt from a short story. How would you describe Aaron's parenting style? ______________________________________

____

Mine

Max parked his tricycle carefully on a small patch of shade alongside the spiked metal fence that surrounded the sprinkler area. The depressed rectangle of soft asphalt was the favored hangout of the pre-school set after the sprinklers had been shut off each day, and little ones were already screaming and scurrying about among the shrinking patches of wet ground under the glare of an intense sun. Behind Max, on a raised cement terrace, young men from the neighborhood played basketball and handball. To either side lay a stretch of benches where old people hunkered over grey checkerboard tables, and young children made the most out of the minimum of a playground. Max stepped back to survey his work. He measured the gap between wheel and curb with his eyes and admired the bright yellow and red Fisher-Price decals emblazoned on its fenders. Satisfied, his mind and eyes wandered through the park to the slides and swings beyond.

From a bench in the shade on the other side, Aaron gazed across at his son between paragraphs. He had been bringing Max to this park every Saturday afternoon for almost a year now, a ritual that they both enjoyed. A slight breeze quivered through the gray streaks in Aaron's black hair and rustled the glossy pages in his hands as he watched Max standing in the bright sunlight, mouthing quietly to himself and pointing contentedly toward the play area, a pint-sized tour guide to ghosts. Their eyes met and the corners of Max's mouth twisted into a grin. He did a steep bank to the left as he tip-toed full speed around the fence toward his father, landing smack between his knees, a hand setting on each. Aaron caressed the soft cinnamon blonde spikes on top of Max's head and returned to his reading.

"I'm thirsty," Max announced, squirmed quietly, stretching onto the tips of his toes.

"Thirsty?" Aaron repeated in lazy, mock surprise, biding for time that he might sit a bit longer enjoying the few shady breezes and the last few paragraphs on Congress's reaction to the president's new economic plan. Max fidgeted patiently.

It was between the last two paragraphs that Aaron happened to look up and see a chubby four-year old with Rita Hayworth sunglasses saddling up on the tricycle and taking off. Her dark face aglow, she banked steeply to the left as she careened full speed around the spiked metal fence. Entering the short ramp and steps down into the sprinkler area, she hit full throttle on the soft asphalt below. Sensing trouble, Aaron returned to his reading. Max turned and saw her doing figure eights behind the fence and he let out a shriek. "Mine!" his finger pointed at her in indignant accusation.

Aaron leaned forward and, observing the general scene in the sprinkler area, patted Max's tensed back. "It's okay, sweetheart. You're not riding it now. You can have it back when she's finished." He reassured himself as well with his caring voice and the calm reasoning of his own words.

"It's mine!" Max shrieked again, his foot stomping angrily on the final word, his finger pointing even more accusingly than before.

Aaron looked at his son's reddened face and once again at the girl. A woman he assumed to be her mother chatted nearby with a friend, sitting on the low gray cement wall that supported the spiked metal fence, their gold and magenta saris glistening in the bright sunlight. "Well why don't you go and ask her for it back?" Max stood silently for a moment between his father's knees, tensed, but deep in thought. "Go and tell her you want your tricycle back. Go ahead," Aaron's voice advised, soothing and gentle.

Max repeated again, "It's mine," his voice a softer whine, the anger on his face shifting to the confusion of the learner. He walked over to the entrance in the fence and hesitated a moment to look back at his father. He stepped inside and stopped at the bottom of the steps. In a tiny voice, full of apprehension, he mouthed the words. The girl continued blissfully on her spree.

b Answer the questions. Explain your answers.

1. How do you think Max feels when he is asking the girl for his bike?
2. How do you think Aaron feels about the way he handled the situation?
3. What would you have done if you were in Aaron's position?
4. How do you think the problem will be resolved?

Grammar

2 Add *would* or *wouldn't* to the sentences. Make any other necessary changes.

1. Aaron and Max come to the park every Saturday.
2. Sometimes Max ride his tricycle while Aaron read the paper.
3. Often young men play basketball nearby.
4. Aaron have gotten the tricycle back himself, but he wanted Max to learn how to resolve problems by himself.
5. You give me my tricycle, please?
6. The girl listen to Max.

3 Find the mistakes in the sentences and correct them.

1. He had always said that he will give me money.
2. The teacher wouldn't never smile at me.
3. Would you like follow me to my office?
4. The family moved to the countryside so that they would have had a better quality of life.
5. She warned us that the job would to be hard.
6. I'd have change jobs earlier if I had realize how easy it was.
7. No matter how hard they tried, the horse wouldn't to leave the stable.
8. Would you to turn the lights off when you've finished?

Reading and writing

4 Read about a childhood memory. Answer the questions on a separate sheet of paper.

1. What experience does she describe?
2. Has she always enjoyed exams?
3. Why was she good at exams when she was younger?
4. What was different about the exams she took when she was in college?

This is a test . . .
I think I might have been sort of a geek when I was very young, because I used to love taking tests, and not many people do that. But I think that's because I did a lot of acting, and so I used to study for tests in the same way that I learned my lines. So when it came to test time, I just wrote out the answers word for word. And that's why I found my ACTs pretty easy. It was only later in life, when I came to do things like university exams, where you have to apply theory, that I learned that you can't always get away with just learning things by memory. I remember that I got very stressed out for my college exams, and I certainly learned the lesson that starting review about three weeks before your exam is not a good idea. So, for me, childhood memories of tests were fun, and I always managed to do well, but later on in life it got a little bit more difficult.

5 Complete the expressions in **bold**. Then match them to the definitions.

____ 1. I think I might have been **sort of a** __________.

____ 2. I just wrote out the answers **word for** __________.

____ 3. It was only __________ **in life,** when I came to do things like . . .

____ 4. . . . that you **can't always** __________ **away with** . . .

____ 5. . . . just **learning things by** __________

____ 6. I got very __________ **out** for my college exams.

____ 7. I certainly __________ **the lesson** that . . .

a. write down every word exactly as you learned or read it
b. it is not sufficient
c. nervous and tense
d. someone who studies hard but doesn't fit in socially
e. learned from experience
f. studying and remembering just the hard facts
g. when I was older

UNIT 10 Review

1 Add one word to complete each sentence.

1. I'm of minds as to whether or not to go to the concert.
2. He's been a little bit in the dumps recently.
3. She was at her end about failing the exam.
4. Try not to get so wound about life. Take it easy.
5. I'm feeling pretty pleased myself for passing my driving test.
6. Now all the tickets are sold out, so we're kicking.

2 Circle the correct words to complete the sentences.

1. They're ____ call us while they're in town.
   a. need to c. might to
   b. bound to
2. We ____ get home because the babysitter is waiting.
   a. 're bound to c. ought to
   b. supposed to
3. It ____ an easy decision to make.
   a. can't have been c. isn't bound to be
   b. couldn't to be
4. They ____ there earlier than we were expecting.
   a. must have got c. would got
   b. mightn't have
5. She ____ us if we had to bring something.
   a. is supposed tell c. would have told
   b. might tell
6. The house ____ need painting, because nobody has lived there for ages.
   a. would have c. is likely to
   b. can't have
7. We ____ expected to do all the work by ourselves.
   a. can't be c. are likely to
   b. ought to
8. We ____ reply to the invitation before July 31.
   a. need c. would have
   b. are supposed to
9. I ____ bring the spare copies after all.
   a. 'm likely c. didn't need to
   b. ought

3 One word in each sentence belongs in another sentence. Cross out those words and write them in the correct sentences.

1. He has a tendency to change on the negative.
2. I'm sure it will all work out well in the long bright.
3. Try looking on the people side.
4. Generally, I see problems as run.
5. There are various techniques you can use to dwell your thought patterns.
6. I tend to trust challenges.

4 Circle the correct choice.

1. We were *outraged/petrified/delighted* when she graduated from college with high grades. We had always hoped that she would do well.
2. He was *furious/ecstatic/delighted* when he realized his wallet had been stolen.
3. They were really *terrified/taken aback/indifferent* when we told them the price. It was obviously a shock.
4. She was simply *thrilled/dumbstruck/uninterested* when she received the flowers. You could tell by her huge smile.
5. I'm a little *delighted/flabbergasted/indifferent* toward classical music. It doesn't do anything for me.
6. Most days she felt *miserable/taken aback/livid*, and longed to see her friends and family at home.
7. I told him all about what had been happening, but he was completely *outraged/uninterested/ecstatic*. He just kept watching TV.
8. She was *terrified/livid/dumbstruck* that her parents would find out what she had been doing.
9. Katia was *livid/thrilled/ecstatic* when she saw the mess that the builders had left. She immediately called the company to complain.

5 Add *would* or *wouldn't* to the story where appropriate.

When I was younger, my parents were always busy. They had just started their own business, so they often had to go overseas and couldn't take care of my brother and me. When they went away on these trips, they send us to stay with my grandfather, a fruit farmer who lives in the foothills of the mountains. I was always happy when my mother told us we stay with Grandpa, since the time we spent at his house was always wonderful. The air there was fresh and clean, and the scenery was beautiful. There was no pollution. In the morning, I wake up and smell the grass and the flowers, and hear the birds singing their song. There was an orchard filled with fruit trees of many kinds, and we were always happy when our grandfather ask: "You like to help pick the fruit?" When the fruit was ripe, we could pick as much as we could eat. And when there was too much, we set up a fruit stand, and make good money selling the sweet fruit to passers-by.

My grandfather kept dogs and chickens, and took us for walks in the forest. Here he taught us the names of the plants, so that we know which were good to eat, which were useful for medicinal purposes, and which were toxic. He let us pick the plants until we could tell him what each one was. We learned so much when we were with him, more than we have learned by going to school. I have stayed there forever, if it were possible.

6 Write five sentences about the story, using *would* or *wouldn't*.

Ex: *When their parents went away, the boys' grandfather would take care of them.*

____

____

____

____

____

***English in Common* ActiveBook**
Installation Instructions

Windows
- Insert the disc into the CD-ROM drive of your computer. On most computers, the program will begin automatically.
- If the program does not begin automatically, open "My Computer."
- Right-click on the CD-ROM icon. Click on Open.

Macintosh
- Insert the disc into the CD-ROM drive of your computer.
- Double-click on the CD-ROM icon on your desktop.
- Double click on the "START_OSX" file to run the program. Leave the CD-ROM in the computer while using the program.

Note: You must have administrator privileges on the computer to install the program. To install:
- **Windows:** Double-click on the "install" file to start the installation.
- **Macintosh:** Copy all files from the CD-ROM to a folder on your hard drive.

ActiveBook System Requirements

	PC Compatible	**Macintosh Compatible**
Operating System	Microsoft Windows® XP, Vista, Windows 7	Mac OSX v. (10.4 & 10.5)
Processor	Intel Pentium® IV 1000MHz or faster processor (or equivalent)	PowerPC & Intel processor 500MHz or faster processor (or equivalent)
RAM	512 MB RAM minimum or higher	512 MB RAM minimum or higher
Internet Browser	Microsoft Internet Explorer® 7.x or Mozilla Firefox™ 4.x, or higher	Safari® 3.x, Mozilla Firefox™ 4.x, or higher
Plug-ins	Adobe PDF 8, Adobe Flash 9, or higher	Adobe PDF 8, Adobe Flash 9, or higher
Hardware	Computer CD-ROM drive, sound card and speakers or headphones	Computer CD-ROM drive, sound card and speakers or headphones
Monitor Resolution	1024x768	1024x768
Internet Connection	DSL, cable/broadband, T1, or other high-speed connection required to download plug-ins	

TECHNICAL SUPPORT
For Technical Product Support, please visit our support website at www.PearsonLongmanSupport.com. You can search our *Knowledgebase* for frequently asked questions, instantly *Chat* with an available support representative, or *Submit a Ticket/Request* for assistance.